More Conversations
on the Porch

Other Books by Beth Lindsay Templeton

Loving Our Neighbor: A Thoughtful Approach to Helping People in Poverty

*Understanding Poverty in the Classroom: Changing
Perceptions for Student Success*

Conversations on the Porch: Ancient Voices—Contemporary Wisdom

A Coat Named Mr. Spot

Angelika's Journal: What You Can Do About Poverty and Homelessness

Refrigerator Prayers for Ordinary People

More Conversations
on the Porch

Ancient Voices—Contemporary Wisdom

Beth Lindsay Templeton

iUniverse LLC
Bloomington

MORE CONVERSATIONS ON THE PORCH
ANCIENT VOICES—CONTEMPORARY WISDOM

iUniverse books may be ordered through booksellers or by contacting:

iUniverse
1663 Liberty Drive
Bloomington, IN 47403
www.iuniverse.com
1-800-Authors (1-800-288-4677)

ISBN: 978-1-4917-2153-7 (sc)
ISBN: 978-1-4917-2154-4 (e)

Library of Congress Control Number: 2014901028

Printed in the United States of America.

iUniverse rev. date: 1/22/2014

For women in ministry in all times and places

Contents

Acknowledgments

More Conversations on the Porch began when the women of Fourth Presbyterian Church in Greenville, South Carolina, asked me to be the speaker at their spring luncheon. I knew that the various women's groups had been using my book, *Conversations on the Porch*, for their Bible study, but I also knew that each group had skipped around in the book. I did not know which women they had visited with. Therefore, I decided to see if another woman wanted to visit with me on the porch. Lady Wisdom arrived. With that began the impetus for this follow-up book. Thank you to all the women at Fourth Presbyterian Church who have encouraged me and invited the women from the Bible to visit with them as well.

Many other groups have used *Conversations on the Porch*, and every time I learn of one, I realize how very blessed I am to be on this journey of faith, inspiration, and discovery. To all the women who have encouraged me to continue to sit on my porch and listen, I say thank you.

I have to thank whoever gave me a first edition of Edith Deen's master work, *All of the Women of the Bible*, Harper and Brothers Publishers, 1955. This book has been on my library shelves for years. Now as the various women come to visit, I consult with Mrs. Deen for her help and guidance. When the book says *all* the women, it really does mean *all* the women!

Thank you to the two different women who asked me within days of each other if there was a woman that I would not write about. I thought and said, "Jezebel." They had planted a seed, because in God's wondrous ways, Jezebel came to life. After the question, Jezebel would not let me go and demanded to be listened to.

Thanks most especially to my husband, who gives me the emotional space to be creative, who challenges me about issues of faith, and who encourages me to follow wherever I feel I'm being led. Jim, you are my true partner in life.

Introduction

The screen porch addition to my house was my gift to myself. All the furniture is shabby. Cushions in the rocking chairs are flat in places. The current green color of the chairs is not original—obviously. Begonias, hostas, and ivies are exuberant in their variety of pots. Wind chimes sing as the breeze tickles the pipes. The three-story magnolia tree just beyond the steps embraces the porch with its wide, old branches. Dinner-plate-size white flowers release their lemony fragrance for all to enjoy.

I created the porch as a sanctuary for me. I realized that I might not always be able to leave town for a getaway but I could always go to the porch and rock. Friends joined me and commented about what a special place it was for them as well. Some admitted it was the only place in the world where they could truly relax. The porch became for many who visited a sacred place where their spirits were nurtured. They found, if not answers, at least signposts for their journeys in life.

It was on this porch that conversations with women from the Bible took place. One summer afternoon, I was sitting there dozing in the warm sun that shone through the screen. As I rocked gently and hummed along with the bees flitting about the magnolia flowers, I realized that I was not alone. A woman sat in the other chair, rocking in rhythm with me. I was shocked at first and thought that perhaps I was hallucinating from the heat. I found my voice and demanded to know who she was. We simply rocked a while longer. Then, somehow, I knew that Eve had come to the porch to share her life and be a guide for my journey. After Eve's visit, others came. I recorded the conversations of the first thirty women in *Conversations on the Porch*. After a while, even more women came. These are their stories in *More Conversations on the Porch*.

Sometimes I would go to the porch having been overwhelmed with the day. Over and over again, the women came to me, sharing their lives, offering their insights, and challenging me with new visions for how to live, what to care about, and how to use my passion and energy.

The women came from their places of power or powerlessness, with their strengths or vulnerabilities, and their successes and failures. Some of the women are considered saints. Others are vilified. They came to the porch to share their insights and guidance. These visitors embraced me with their wisdom, their love, and their passion. They rocked in the chairs and asked that whoever would hear their stories would listen. They are depending on us to hear their ancient voices as we move into our own renewed and expanded visions of life as people of God. They challenge us to embrace living as they did and to continue the conversations.

I've been asked if the women appeared "bodily as with flesh and blood." That's a difficult question. To me, each woman was real. Whether she was visible to the eye or only to my heart and mind is inconsequential to the wisdom she shared. You can determine for yourself the answer to this question.

How to Use This Book

The first book, *Conversations on the Porch*, had thirty chapters. Some Bible-study groups used one or two chapters a month for a school year. Others met weekly. Some groups decided to spend two years working through the chapters. They skipped around or went in the order of the women as presented. They visited with all the women or chose only a representative group. Some individuals have read one chapter a day for a month.

There is no right or wrong way to use this book. Just as the women came to me in no particular order, you can choose to read the chapters in whatever way speaks to you.

More Conversations on the Porch has twelve chapters and an additional bonus chapter so that you or a group can use one chapter a month for a year or one a week for three months. The bonus chapter is just that—one to use or not.

If you are studying this book in a group, you may want to ask someone to read the chapter aloud. Encourage group members to listen to the story rather than following along in their books. In this way, they will hear the story as the woman told it.

Questions for discussion along with a reminder of the call(s) to action that the guest issued during her visit immediately follow each conversation. Please consider these in light of your own experiences and expectations. If you are reading *More Conversations on the Porch* by yourself, you may want to record your thoughts and feelings in a journal. If you are using this book in a group, discuss the questions that are relevant for you.

It is my hope that you will find the conversations with these biblical women as challenging and encouraging as I did.

Blessings,

Beth
November, 2013

Chapter One

Abigail—Courage and Change

I Samuel 25:2–42; 30:5,18; I Chronicles 3:1

Abigail was first married to Nabal but later became the wife of King David.

I had been on the porch for most of the afternoon reading my novel. It was one of those books that are often in stores on the table with a sign saying Beach Reads. I've never enjoyed lying out on the beach baking in the sun and reading. However, I thoroughly enjoy taking a mini-vacation on my porch and reading away a relaxing Sunday afternoon. I had just finished my novel, content that the main characters had found resolution to their problems and even had experienced some hope. It was a totally satisfying escape experience. Almost as soon as I put the book down, I realized that I had a visitor.

I looked over at a beautiful woman sitting in the rocking chair beside me. She was dressed in a lovely green dress that fit her perfectly. Her tawny hair was arranged in an old-fashioned style, wrapped around her head laced with cords of green and gold. Her feet had golden sandals. Bracelets that were both simple and elegant adorned both her arms. I was speechless in the presence of this lovely lady.

I bowed my head to her and said, almost in a whisper, "Welcome."

She said, "Thank you. My name is Abigail."

I responded, "I am honored to have you as a guest." All the while I was thinking, *Abigail? Who is Abigail?*

I said, "Other women have visited me on this porch. I treasure what they shared with me from their life experiences. I value the wisdom they offered and the insights they told me about loving and living fully. Do you have such a story as well?"

Abigail replied, "Yes, I do."

She began, "I was married to a man named Nabal. He was very wealthy but mean. Some say he was surly. King David sent emissaries to my husband to let him know that David's men had been providing protection for our shearers while they were working with the sheep. David's men came offering peace and asking for food for the troops. My foolish husband retorted that he didn't know who these people were and that he wasn't going to give them any food or drink. He added that they could go back where they came from.

"Some of the servants who were loyal to me came and told me what had happened. They said that David's men had protected them and threatened no harm. However, there was no reasoning with my ill-tempered husband. The servants informed me that because of my husband's harsh retort, David was now planning to kill the entire household of Nabal.

"I knew that I was married to a difficult man, but this kind of behavior was simply too much. I told my young male servants to return to David and that I would follow shortly. But I did not mention a thing to Nabal. You can't talk or reason with someone like him. I had already learned that lesson myself from the abusive treatment I had suffered at his hands.

"I asked one of my servants to prepare a donkey for me to ride and to gather two hundred loaves of bread, two skins of wine, five sheep ready to be dressed, five measures of grain, and lots of raisins and figs. I rode out to meet David. I was careful to stay within the shadows of Mount Carmel because I did not want my foul-mouthed husband to discover what I was doing.

"I later learned that when David saw us coming, he told God that he'd kill all the men who belonged to Nabal because my foolish husband had not appreciated David's protection of our men in the wilderness. Fortunately I got to David before he was able to implement his plan.

"I went as fast as I could get my donkey to move. All the while, I thought about what I could say to this powerful man. As soon as I saw David, I hurried my donkey toward him, jumped off, and bowed immediately to the ground.

I said, 'Let me take the blame for this travesty. I'm married to a harsh man. I did not see your emissaries; otherwise, I would have made sure to honor their request for food. Please do not kill our household, because that would be a dishonor to the Lord. I know that you follow the Lord God Almighty and that you do not want to do evil. I do not want you to suffer grief or have pangs of conscience because you sought vengeance by your own hand. Please allow me, your servant, to make right what should have been done.'

"The words that David said to me were blessings to my ears. He said, 'Blessed be the Lord, the God of Israel, who sent you to meet me today! Blessed be your good sense, and blessed be you, who have kept me today from blood-guilt and from avenging myself by my own hand!' (I Samuel 25:33). Isn't that something? David called me a woman of good sense.

"It was wonderful to be appreciated for my actions. Certainly I'd never received any kind of affirmation or affection from my husband, but here was David, anointed by Samuel, admiring me. I encourage you to be brave and do what is right, especially when other lives are at risk. Had Nabal discovered my plan, he surely would have killed me. Had I not taken this chance, all of our household, through no fault of their own, would have been murdered. I encourage you to step outside of expected cultural norms when it's important. Praise God, I'm glad I did, because I was able to save the lives of everyone who worked and lived with us.

"Well, not quite all our household survived. When I returned home, I planned to tell Nabal what I'd done, but he was partying and was quite drunk. I decided to wait until the morning when he'd recovered from his festivities. The next day, after he'd slept off his hangover, I went to my husband and told him about my visit with David. He was so enraged that he literally had a stroke and fell over paralyzed. He died ten days later.

"This is not the end of the story, however.

"David heard about what happened to my husband. He praised God for dealing with Nabal's evildoing and for keeping David from taking matters into his own hands. He remembered me. David, soon to be king over all of Israel, remembered me! He sent for me and wooed me. I became his wife along with Ahinoham of Jezreel. His first wife, Michal, who had been given to David by King Saul, had by now been given by her father to Paltison from Galim.

"I suspect that you might find it strange that David took me and Ahinoham as wives at the same time. This really was not so odd in our era. We women were given in marriage to solidify political claims rather than for what you might call love.

"My relationship with David was not a political liaison, however. As I told you, David admired my good sense. When he learned of Nabal's death, David courted me by sending his servants to me. No man gave me to David. I *gave myself* because I chose to. David was a man I was proud to be linked with. He was not foolish and ill-tempered like my first husband. I was thrilled to be chosen as his wife. Can you imagine how heady my life was? I freely gave myself to the king because he wanted me. Me! It seemed like a fairy tale.

"Fairy tales, however, have dark sides to them. We lived in Ziglag. One day while David was fighting battles elsewhere, the Amalekites came to the Negeb and attacked Ziglag. They took all the women and children captive, including Ahinoham and me. We were terrified. None of us knew what might happen to us. We whispered that we did not know if we'd rather be killed or put into slavery. We huddled together and tried to keep up each other's spirits. We prayed for deliverance from our Lord. We sang words that we'd heard our husband sing. One of the songs goes like this: 'In you, O Lord, I seek refuge; do not let me ever be put to shame; in your righteousness deliver me. Incline your ear to me; rescue me speedily. Be a rock of refuge for me, a strong fortress to save me' (Psalm 31:1–2). As I lay huddled in the night with Ahinoham, I sometimes wondered if it might have been better for me to have died at David's hand when he decided to kill Nabal and our household. I had now known the joy of being married to a man I admired rather than one I detested. The possibility of losing that deep satisfaction caused me tremendous grief.

"Unbeknownst to us, David had captured a young man of Egypt who had been fighting with the Amalekites. They had abandoned him on the side of the road because he was sick. David fed him and nursed him back to strength. In gratitude, the young man told David about the raiding party on Ziglag. David swore that he would not harm the Egyptian if he would show him where this raiding party was. That's how David found us.

4

"First he attacked the Amalekites who were celebrating their victory and spoils. It took David the entire night, but he killed all of the men except for four hundred who escaped on camels. After the battle, David discovered every person and every item that had been taken from Ziglag. When he rescued Ahinoham and me, we fell on him with kisses all over his feet. He seemed pleased but pushed us off, saying he had other people and things to collect.

"When we all returned to Ziglag, my wonderful husband shared the spoils with our surrounding neighbors. David sent treasure everywhere he had roamed. This was a generous thing to do but also very strategic. After all, he was on his way to consolidating his entire kingdom of Israel. He too had plenty of good sense.

"This fairy tale has one more dark turn. Her name was Bathsheba. This woman stole my husband's heart. She too was a widow, but unlike my first husband, hers was a good and honorable man. David was responsible in certain ways for the deaths of both our husbands—mine because he had a stroke when I told him of my intervention with David, hers because David sent him to the front lines of battle. We both gave him sons. I gave him Daniel, and she gave him Solomon.

"Can you imagine how painful it was to know that my son, the second born, had no claim to the throne? Bathsheba's son, Solomon, who was much farther down the birth line, was the king's designated successor. Can you feel what it was like to have been admired for my wisdom and attractiveness only to be usurped in my husband's life by that woman?

"The fairy tale lost its luster when we moved into a palace in Jerusalem. Many of David's sons grew and began vying for the throne. With great power comes great peril. So my life took many twists and turns, some pleasant and some painful. I urge you to use your mind to help others. Remember that the bad times will not last forever. I did not have to remain yoked to awful Nabal, nor did I end up a slave of the Amalekites. But the good times do not last either. My status as wife grew less and less as David's power grew more and more. When he and I married, he was still thought of by many as an outlaw, a fugitive. When he became king over all of Israel, our lives changed. I admit I long for the days before Jerusalem.

"My call to you is to remember that life is full of changes. Take <u>risks</u> when they are required to protect others. Remember that getting to live in a palace is <u>not</u> all that you think it will be."

With those final words, Abigail left the porch.

Reflecting on Abigail's Visit

1. Abigail said to step outside of cultural norms when it's important to do so.

   * Have you ever had to step beyond cultural norms? If so, what were the challenges? What were the benefits?
   * Was there a time when you were challenged to step beyond cultural norms and you did not? What held you back?
   * How can you know when it is important to move beyond the norms?

2. Abigail said to remember that life is full of changes.

   * Do you agree or disagree?
   * Are all changes either good or bad? Are some changes both good and bad?
   * How does remembering that life is full of challenges help or hinder your journey?

3. Abigail said to take risks when they are required to protect others.

   * Have you ever done this? When? What was your experience with that?
   * Have you ever not taken risks and later on wished you had? What stopped you? What changed how you thought about the situation?
   * What criteria would you use to decide if a risk is worth taking?

4. Abigail said to remember that getting to live in a palace is not all you think it will be.

   * Does this challenge you in your own life or community? If so, how?
   * Does Abigail's journey stir up a story for you? If so, what?
   * Did you learn anything from listening to Abigail?

<u>Advice:</u> * Does her story inspire you to action? If so, what? When? How? Why?

"Bring up touchy subjects at opportune times." Pray⁶ for guidance!

Chapter Two

Jezebel—Misguided Beliefs

I Kings 16; 18–19; 21; II Kings 9

Jezebel was married to King Ahab. She introduced the worship of pagan gods into Israel. She and Elijah contended with each other.

Occasionally a volunteer or a supporter of the nonprofit where I used to work would tell me about a new project or a new nonprofit in town. Sometimes representatives from the start-up group wanted to meet with me for my advice or my opinion. Other times they simply wanted to let me know what they were planning. Usually I listened, offered whatever insights I had, and tried to help the new group avoid some of the mistakes that I had made.

There were some groups, however, that I thought were just wrong. I felt as if they might be exploiting the people they were trying to help. When I heard their plans, I wondered who they were trying to benefit—themselves or the people they professed they wanted to help. When I felt strongly about an organization that was trying to get started, I would be a strong naysayer or a strong advocate, depending on what I believed was happening.

One organization really irritated me even though its proponents were people whom I admired and trusted. I tried to relay my misgivings in positive and constructive ways. Nevertheless, I lost some rapport. Some of the people involved certainly did not like me very much.

The organization began and, in the first years, confirmed my fears about what would happen.

But then I began hearing from volunteers who worked in the program about how powerful they believed it was. They told how getting involved in that organization had opened their eyes to deeper issues of poverty. They excitedly shared how their congregation was now involved in poverty remediation in meaningful ways.

The organization had a change in staff and added components that moved people from basic relief of their poverty to being able to address their long-term goals. Program participants now had the opportunity to develop financial stability in their lives. I begin to speak publicly in favor of the organization.

I was sitting on the porch thinking about how *right* I had thought I was. Now, some years later, I realized that although I may have had some valid concerns, I was ultimately wrong in my long-term assessment. That's not easy to admit. I probably lost the respect of some people forever.

A woman appeared in the chair beside me. I knew she was there even before I looked over. Her presence was dominating and even threatening. I felt myself pull inward. My uneasiness made me reluctant to ask her name, but finally I spoke, even though my voice trembled: "Hello. Who are you?"

She turned her face toward me with an imperious look and said haughtily, "My name is Jezebel!"

I must have fallen back deeper into my chair and responded with a less than welcoming look, because she said, "Are you *not* happy with my presence here?"

I looked up at the ceiling and thought to myself, *I don't really want this infamous woman sitting here on my porch. What if someone sees her? What will they think of me?* But then I thought about what a wonderful opportunity I had to discover more about this woman whose name is almost synonymous with wickedness.

I replied, "To be truthful, you are probably the last woman whom I would have expected to come to this porch to talk with me. However, since you are here, you must have some wisdom to share with me. I feel I must remind you that I am a Christian, and I know that you worship the pagan gods Baal and Asherah, so let's agree that I will not try to convert you and you will not try to convert me. Okay?"

She huffed and agreed to my proposal. She said, "I'll adhere to your request because you're allowing me to be a guest on your porch. I usually do not agree to others' demands. I guess you already know what happened between Elijah, your God's prophet, and my prophets and family?"

I nodded but said, "I'd like to hear your version of what happened."

She began. "My father, king of Tyre, gave me as a bride for Ahab to Ahab's father, King Omri of Israel. This was a political marriage to solidify the relationship between Israel and Phoenicia against Syria. The marriage was celebrated in a lavish manner. A song was composed for our wedding. I still remember some of the words: 'You are the most handsome of men; grace is poured upon your lips … In your majesty ride on victoriously for the cause of truth and to defend the right … From ivory palaces stringed instruments make you glad; daughters of kings are among your ladies of honor … Hear, O daughter, consider and incline your ear; forget your people and your father's house, and the king will desire your beauty … The princess is decked in her chamber with gold-woven robes; in many-colored robes she is led to the king … With joy and gladness they are led along as they enter the palace of the king' (Psalm 45:2,4,8-11,13,15).

"I tried to do honor to my husband. I brought 450 prophets of Baal and 400 prophets of the mother-goddess Asherah with me so the land would be fertile. I wanted to help the peasants who were struggling so hard to bring harvest from their fields. I believed my fertility gods could do that. I even asked Ahab to build the prophets a home near ours so that their influence could be strong for my husband and my new country. I believed we would all prosper. What did I get for all my efforts? Well, I'll tell you.

"We were having a terrible drought in Samaria. Elijah, that terrible little prophet of the Lord of Israel and Judah, said that the drought was because my husband, King Ahab, had built temples and altars for my gods, Baal and Asherah. As I said, the peasants of Israel were happy to have my gods helping them with their farming tasks. But Elijah, that horrible and ugly man, said that his God had caused the drought to prove once and for all that my gods were powerless.

"I knew that my husband was weak and would do nothing. Even though he allowed my gods to be worshiped in Israel in order to make me happy, he was afraid to totally abandon the God of his youth. I was tired of the

9

dire comments of Elijah and the prophets of the God of Israel. I wanted to clear the land for the gods whom I worshiped; therefore, I had God's prophets killed.

"After Elijah told Ahab that the Lord had caused the drought, the troublemaker went into hiding. I was furious. I told Ahab to find Elijah, but nothing happened for about three years until Elijah came out of hiding and challenged my prophets to a show of power.

"I was not there but later heard what happened. Elijah proposed that two bulls would be sacrificed on top of Mount Carmel. My prophets, those of Baal, built an altar and laid a fire. Elijah did the same thing. Whichever god first caused the bull to burn on the altar and be consumed as a sacrifice would be the true god.

"All of my 450 prophets of Baal and 400 prophets of Asherah were there. They had elaborately prepared their sacrifice and had the first choice of bulls. They processed around the altar and chanted and exhorted. They called on Baal and Asherah, but there was no fire. By late morning, their chants were not as strong.

"Elijah taunted them. He called out, 'Speak louder. Maybe your gods can't hear you or they are asleep. Wake them up. Maybe they are daydreaming.' This just enraged my prophets, so they began to scream and cut themselves, spilling their own blood as sacrifice. But nothing happened with the fire and the sacrificial bull.

"Then it was Elijah's turn. He made a big show and told servants to dig a trench around his altar and to pour water on the wood for the fire—not one time but three times. They poured so much water on the altar that the trench was filled. Then Elijah prayed. He did not march around or chant or do any of the things that my Baal prophets did. He simply prayed. I heard that he asked the God of Israel to do this thing so people would realize who the true God was. And there was fire. Everything was burned up, even the stones of the altar. The people fell down and worshiped.

"Next Elijah did an unforgiveable act as far as I was concerned. He ordered all the prophets of Baal to be killed. Then he told Ahab to go get something to eat while Elijah worshiped God and his servant watched the sky for signs of rain. After that, Elijah told my husband he'd better hurry home before it started raining. Elijah ran and jumped for joy alongside Ahab's chariot. My stupid husband did exactly what that little man told him to do. And what happened next? It started raining!"

I asked Jezebel, "Did you consider worshiping the God of Israel then?"

She said, "What? Of course not! I had been raised to revere Baal and Asherah. They had gotten me where I was, the wife of a king, weak though he was. Why in the world would I want to worship any other gods?"

I dared not say these things to Jezebel, but I wondered to myself what it would take for someone to let go of the lessons of youth in order to grow into a maturity different from what had been imagined. What would have happened if Jezebel had seen the God of Israel as the powerful God that Elijah had demonstrated that day? Why is it so hard for people to let go of their childhood lessons when other truths are so obvious?

We sat in silence for a bit. I was curious about what Jezebel was thinking. She surprised me when she said, "From where I sit now in history, I wonder how things might have been different if I could have renounced my gods for the God of the land where I lived. A lot of death and grief followed me. But I *knew* that I was right. I realized quickly that I was married to a very weak man. I wanted to be remembered for saving Israel from its folly, not for destroying it. Is this something you struggle with? If so, I hope that you will pay attention to what I tell you and then do things differently."

I looked at her with amazement as I realized that I had just been given a glimpse of the woman behind the stories and hate-filled language. However, before I began to feel too tender toward her, Jezebel said, "Well, I couldn't find Elijah. I had sworn that I would kill him, but once again he went into hiding.

"As I mentioned, my husband, Ahab, was a weak man. Here is an example. Next to our palace was a beautiful vineyard owned by a man named Naboth. The vineyard was perfectly located to be a vegetable garden for the palace. We had a lot of people living in our beautiful house, which was inlaid with ivory. We needed more garden space so we could feed them all. Ahab went to Naboth and offered to buy the land from him, and he even offered to give Naboth another, even better, vineyard. This was a fair and honorable offer.

"Naboth, however, quoted an ancient rule about how his land had been given to him by God for him and his descendants. He could not sell the land because of the ancestral inheritance laws. I thought this was just stupid. The king—the king himself—wanted the land. Who was Naboth to refuse? But my husband did not argue. What did he do? He came to his bed, lay there sulking, and refused to eat.

"When I heard about this, I went to Ahab and said, 'Do you now govern Israel? Get up, eat some food, and be cheerful; I will give you the vineyard of Naboth the Jezreelite' (I Kings 21:7). So I forged some documents in the king's name and created a ruse to discredit Naboth in front of his friends. He and all his family were stoned to death. Now the ancestral inheritance laws were not important, because there were no longer any inheritors.

"I was very proud of myself. I had helped my husband with his little problem. I assumed he would be very pleased with me. But no, once again that detestable man Elijah showed up when Ahab was at the vineyard claiming it for his own. One of the servants later reported to me that Elijah placed a curse on Ahab and Ahab's entire household and even his descendants. According to the servant, Elijah said, 'Thus says the Lord: In the place where dogs licked up the blood of Naboth, dogs will also lick up your blood … I will bring disaster on you; I will consume you, and will cut off from Ahab every male, bond or free, in Israel … Also … the Lord said, "The dogs shall eat Jezebel within the bounds of Jezreel. Anyone belonging to Ahab who dies in the city the dogs shall eat; and anyone of his who dies in the open country the birds of the air shall eat" (I Kings 21:19, 21, 23–24).

"When Ahab heard Elijah, he became very afraid and dressed in sackcloth and fasted. He walked around dejectedly. Elijah reported that God said that since Ahab was remorseful, nothing would happen as long as Ahab was alive but the curses would come upon our sons and the rest of Ahab's household upon Ahab's death."

As I rocked and listened, I was entranced by this story. I imagined it as a movie on the big screen. It had it all: romance, deception, special effects, and murder. I had to concentrate not to go too far in my own imagination. So I asked, "What happened next?"

Jezebel's face changed. I saw a flash of pain and grief pass over her eyes. She quickly recovered, however, and her regal, haughty mask was once again in place. She continued, "For about three years, nothing happened. However, Ahab went to battle in alliance with King Jehoshaphat of Judah and died in the field. His soldiers put his body in a chariot and brought it back to Samaria. They washed my husband's blood off the chariot, and true to Elijah's prophecy, the dogs licked up his blood and prostitutes bathed in the water.

"My son Ahaziah reigned two years after his father's death, but he fell from his upper chamber. As he lay on his bed, he sent messengers to Baalzebub to ask if he would live. The messengers came instead upon Elijah, who said that Ahaziah would never leave his bed but would die. Ahaziah asked the messengers to describe this man who said these things and realized that once again Elijah was causing problems. Indeed, my son died as Elijah had said.

"Then my son Joram succeeded to the throne in Israel and reigned for twelve years. Elisha, the successor of Elijah, anointed Jehu, son of Jehoshaphat, as king even while my son was reigning. Jehu battled with my son and King Ahaziah of Judah on the fields of Naboth the Jezreelite, and there my son died. His blood soaked the fields of Naboth just as Elijah had prophesied. Jehu also killed King Athaliah of Judah, who was a descendent of my father-in-law, King Omri of Israel. I had been very fond of Athaliah because he was very much like his uncle, my husband, Ahab.

"Then Jehu came to Jezreel. When I learned that he was on his way to my home, I put on my most beautiful clothes and my finest makeup and looked out the window at Jehu. I called out to him, hoping to win him over, but he told the eunuchs with me to throw me out the window. They did. By the time someone thought to get my body to bury me, the dogs had eaten most of me, and only my skull, feet, and hands were left. Jehu continued his bloody conquest by having the heads of Ahab's sons, all seventy of them, brought to him in a basket. He cleared the land of all of us."

I sat in my rocking chair and did not know what to say. This bloodbath was almost more than I could listen to, and yet I wanted to see if Jezebel had learned anything from all this. Was there anything decent about her?

I waited to see what else she might add. When she said nothing, I noted, "You had a horrific death."

She looked at me in astonishment and said, "I suppose I did. I lived in a time of warring, intrigue, and battle. I lived in a time when women followed the decisions and control of men. However, I was a strong and powerful woman. I was raised in a political family. I devoutly worshiped the gods of my homeland. I did what I thought was right for my adopted country and my family. It turns out that I was very wrong. I could not see that while I was alive. Now, only as I tell my story, I see where I brought to my family much of the tragedy that we suffered. How could I have known?"

I asked her, "Given what you know now, do you have any words of wisdom for me?"

Jezebel replied, "Yes, I'd say to be true to your beliefs but not dogmatic. If you can, listen to others who may have a different truth from yours. I know that if I had been able to do that, some of my family might still be alive."

And with those final words, she left.

I took a deep breath and decided to go inside to take a bath. I felt very dirty after Jezebel's visit. I knew that her words would haunt me for a long time.

Reflecting on Jezebel's Visit

1. Jezebel said to be true to your beliefs but not dogmatic. If you can, listen to others who may have a different truth from yours.

    -   How would Jezebel's life have been different if she had followed her own advice?
    -   Have you ever changed your mind about something that you at first felt strongly about? How did that affect your life?
    -   How can you discern when another's truth has value to you, especially if it seems to contradict your own?

2. I dared not say these things to Jezebel, but I wondered to myself what it would take for someone to let go of the lessons of youth in order to grow into a maturity different from what had been imagined.

    -   How does one let go of childhood beliefs when appropriate?
    -   Do you have examples of outgrown childhood beliefs?
    -   Why is it so hard for people to let go of their childhood lessons when other truths are obvious?

3. Jezebel said that she did what she thought was right for her adopted country and her family. It turns out that she was very wrong.

- ✦ Has this been your challenge? If so, how did you handle it?
- ✦ Does Jezebel's visit change how you think about her? If so, how?
- ✦ Does her story stir up a story for you? If so, what?
- ✦ What did you learn from listening to Jezebel?

Chapter Three

Joanna—Finding Your Way

Luke 8:3; Luke 24:1–12; Acts 1:12–26

Joanna was a follower of Jesus.

I was sitting on the porch thinking about a friend of mine who had recently lost her job. She was actively searching for employment, but nothing seemed to be happening. She was trying to figure out what her next move might be. She could not decide if she wanted to continue doing what she'd been doing or if God was calling her to use other experiences, life passions, and interests in new ways that would cover her living expenses. Did she want just a job or a career? She had submitted numerous applications and had even been called in for a few interviews, but nothing was falling into place.

She was beginning to feel a bit desperate. I could listen to her, give her job leads as I learned of positions, and pray for her, but I was unable to make those doors to employment open for her as she yearned for them to. Even though she was depending on God's guidance, she was scared.

I was holding my friend in prayer while I rocked on the porch. That was all I could do with my own frustration over her situation. Life just didn't seem very fair for her right now. I was beginning to get worked up not only over the difficulty of her situation but also over the realities of other friends who were unemployed, in jobs they disliked, or were searching for what they were *supposed* to do with their lives.

As I rocked faster and faster, I realized that I had a guest. I looked over toward the other rocking chair and said, "Hi. Who are you?"

"I'm Joanna."

I replied, "I'm sorry; I'm not sure that I remember you."

The woman nodded and said gently, "Maybe not. I'm only mentioned a few times in the New Testament and always with someone else."

"Oh." I still was puzzled.

She began, "I guess I need to introduce myself better. My name is Joanna, which means 'Yahweh's gift.' I was married to Chuza, who was a steward in Herod's palace. I'll tell you more about that in a bit. I was healed by Jesus and became one of the women who traveled with him and helped to provide support for his ministry and our journey. I was also with Mary of Magdala and a few other women who found the tomb empty after that horrible time. I later moved to Rome with my new husband, Andronicus, but changed my name from its Hebrew version, Joanna, to its Latin form, Junia."

I exclaimed, "Wow. You must have some wisdom and insights to share."

She nodded and said, "Yes, I suppose I do.

"As I mentioned, I was married to Chuza. We lived in Tiberias as part of the household of Herod. The tetrarch was the son of Herod the Great, who ordered all those dear baby boys killed when the star appeared in the east. He knew that the star was a sign of something that might ultimately threaten his kingdom. When he died, his three sons split up his kingdom, and Herod Antipas got Judah.

"Life in the palace was … what shall I say … interesting? Chuza and I are Jewish, but being in the palace meant that we were privileged beyond the simple means of most of our fellow countrymen. In fact, most of our relatives and childhood friends hated us because Chuza, being responsible for the household affairs of Herod, had to oversee the taxation of all citizens. While we lived in luxury, our neighbors lived a day-to-day existence.

"Herod was a stupid man. He fell prey to the wiles of his brother's wife, Herodias, and so he married her. She, in turn, hated John, who baptized people, because he had criticized her so-called marriage with Herod, her brother-in-law. She plotted along with her daughter to have John killed.

When I heard the chatter in the palace about what had happened, I was horrified. I think that was a wake-up call for me. If a fellow Jew could be beheaded right in the palace where I'd been living so complacently, then how safe, really, were Chuza and I?

"I worried and worried about our future so much that I began to lose my mind, I guess you'd say today. Chuza was not as concerned as I was. He liked his power and authority that he wielded as chief steward. I, on the other hand, began to fall apart, not caring for my appearance, crying uncontrollably, and not eating.

"The wife of one of the common people who delivered fruits to the household saw me one day sitting on a wall in the courtyard, pulling at my hair and weeping uncontrollably. Even though it was dangerous for her to do so, she approached me and asked if she could do something for me. I sobbed even more and said, 'No. My life is over.'

"She continued to look at me. I finally raised my eyes and looked into hers. They were so kind and full of compassion. I must have looked confused as I regarded her through my tears.

"She whispered, 'My lady, your life is not over. Maybe I should not speak of this, but there is a rabbi who is wandering the countryside healing people and preaching the love of our holy God. I have heard him speak. Since my encounter with him, I have been filled with joy and peace. Maybe he could heal you.'

"That gentle woman who risked her life to talk with me became the catalyst for the next chapter in my life. I began to listen more closely to the Jewish tradespeople who came in and out of the palace. I learned that the name of this rabbi was Jesus. Still I cried and my hair was matted and my clothes were unkempt.

"One day, I slipped out of the palace and walked with some of the peasants to the area where Jesus was reported to be preaching. Without going into detail, that connection with Jesus healed my spirit, and I began to believe that my life was not over and could have meaning beyond living in the palace of Herod.

"I spoke with Chuza about what I had experienced. He was understandably distressed. After all, he was a respected and responsible member of Herod's household. Herod had killed John the Baptist. What would he to do to his chief steward when he found out that his steward's wife was now becoming a follower of Jesus, who was connected with the man he had beheaded?

"Chuza loved me, but he loved his position more. He divorced me. However, he gave me my dowry, which was sizable. He was not required by law to do this, but he wanted to take care of me even while protecting himself. I understood his position and thanked him for giving me my freedom. Nevertheless, I was scared beyond any fear I'd ever experienced and yet was amazingly at peace with what was happening.

"So I left the palace with all its security and grandeur and found Jesus and his disciples. I joined the women who followed him and offered my dowry to help provide for all of us.

"I don't know what I expected. I guess I thought that the disciples would embrace me with grateful joy because I was able to lighten their burden through my care and resources. I was wrong, however. They looked on me with suspicion. After all, I came from the political system that had beheaded John the Baptist. I belonged to the world of Herod, who made their lives miserable with his excessive taxation and resentment of their religious practices. They thought I was a spy or worse. Some probably thought I was a bored, wealthy woman who was trying to find some excitement in her life.

"The women in the group, though, understood my passion and commitment. Some of them also provided for the care of our little band. We talked as we cooked and cleaned. We each had left our former lives and cast our lot with this man, Jesus. It was highly unusual for women to leave their homes and families to follow an itinerant preacher like we were doing. Those of us with resources were considered even more suspect. Nevertheless, we knew that we were where we belonged. We knew that even though our world seemed upside down from the way we were all raised, we were doing exactly what Jesus needed and wanted us to do. That was all that mattered.

"I tell you this part of my story to encourage to you to move beyond cultural expectations when you are serving our Lord. No matter what the etiquette books say or what your family members tell you is the right thing for you, when you know and love Jesus, all those things are no longer important. You do what your heart leads you to do because of the love you feel for Jesus and because of his love for you.

"Does that make sense? Some may answer no, but for me that question deserves a resounding yes—yes to Jesus, yes to yourself, and yes to meaning and life.

"We traveled the countryside with Jesus. His teachings and healings continued to excite and challenge us. We were not sure what our futures held. It really didn't matter, because we were with him. Life was hard, but we did not mind. We felt we were part of something bigger than ourselves. We talked in the evenings when Jesus went away from us to pray. We tried to discern what was going to happen. Mostly the women listened while the men argued about this and that. Some thought that Jesus was going to overthrow the Romans. Others thought that the crowds would raise him up as their leader, because everywhere we went multitudes followed. Some of us puzzled about the things Jesus said to us, things that now, as we look back, were his way of trying to prepare us for what was coming. But we were thickheaded and caught up in the travels, the crowds, the teachings, and the healings.

"Then we went to Jerusalem. Because we women were not allowed into certain areas of the Temple, we depended on what the men told us. I suppose you've heard about Jesus's interaction with the moneychangers when he overturned their tables in the Temple. At first, that did not seem like the Jesus we knew, but then when we learned that he'd said, 'It is written, "My house shall be called a house of prayer; but you are making it a den of robbers"' (Matthew 21:13), we began to understand that this man was more than a teacher. He was also a prophet who needed to do dramatic things for us to hear God's message to us.

"When he was crucified, I was one of the women who stood by the cross. Most of the men were not there. But we women were—as always— there to do whatever we could to relieve his sufferings. This time, we were helpless to comfort him or help him rest. After that gruesome death, we wondered what was going to happen next. We were not sure that the men would allow us to continue to travel with them. We were not even sure if the men would continue in the Jesus way. Maybe they would go back to their jobs as fishermen or tax collectors or the other worlds that Jesus had plucked them from.

"I had my own special grief to bear when I heard of Herod's role in the murder of Jesus. I wondered what was going on with Chuza in all of this. Did he even know what had happened? Was he there? Was he safe? Was he afraid? Of course, I never found out the answers to these questions. Our lives were no longer linked, but because of my time in the palace, I felt shame with what had happened—as if I were in some way responsible. I know that's probably crazy, but I had not been out of that life for very long and … I can't go on."

Joanna sighed and rocked while she composed herself again.

"We women were especially concerned about what was going to happen to us after Jesus's death. In following him, we had cut ourselves off from being able to return to our former lives. We were truly on our own, not a comfortable place to be. Before we could deal with what was next for us, we had one more task to do for our Lord. We had to wrap his broken body in spices and ointments.

"We went to the tomb—Mary of Magdala, James's mother Mary, some other women, and me. We found the tomb empty of his body, but these dazzling creatures of light told us that Jesus had risen from the dead. They reminded us of Jesus's teaching that he would be handed over to sinners to be crucified and that he would rise on the third day. We remembered then.

"We hurried back to the disciples to tell them the good news, but they looked at us as if we were suffering from heat stroke. You would have thought we were speaking gibberish from the way they reacted to us. Of course, eventually, they too came to believe."

Joanna once again became silent as she remembered that time. Then she continued.

"I was part of the group who helped choose the replacement for Judas, the traitor. We were all in Jerusalem praying on Mount Olivet. Peter said that we had to choose another, someone who had been with us from the day of Jesus's baptism. The new apostle had to have seen Jesus after the resurrection. The names of two different men were put forth, and the apostles cast lots. Matthias was chosen.

"I began to share what I knew about Jesus to whoever would listen. Life was different, of course, from when Jesus was with us. We all were changed, each in our own way.

"Because I was comfortable being around Romans, having lived in Herod's temple, I was at ease meeting people who were educated, had political responsibilities, or were not Jewish. When I met Andronicus, I knew that we connected in a way that was special. Andronicus too was a follower of Jesus. We shared our lives and our love because of who Jesus was in our individual journeys. After we became husband and wife, we met Paul and decided to travel with him to help spread Jesus's gospel throughout the gentile world. This made sense to us because both of us had life experiences that made us uniquely ready to talk with people who were not Jews but whose hearts had been prepared by the Holy Spirit to accept the teachings of our Lord. We traveled around the region and even went to Rome with Paul. He embraced us as fellow workers for our Lord because we had been with Christ even before Paul met our Savior on that road to Damascus.

"So what can I offer to you from my life story? Be willing to leave your comfort and security when Jesus calls. I left Herod's palace when I knew that following Jesus was the only thing that made sense to me. Also, even when you are not accepted in your role of sharing your faith because of your background—remember the disciples thought I might be a spy—do it anyway. I urge you, when the future seems unknown to you as it did to me after Jesus's murder, to trust in the Lord that your path will unfold according to God's plan. Who could have predicted that I would meet Andronicus and we would marry and become missionaries with Paul? And finally, remember that whatever your life journey and circumstances are, those particular experiences are exactly what make you unique in God's plan for the world. Embrace your history as you live into God's future."

"Dear Joanna, I'm so glad that you came for a visit. Thank you for sharing your very special and unique story with me. I'll remember your encouragements to me."

With that, she was gone.

Reflecting on Joanna's Visit

1. Joanna encouraged us to move beyond cultural expectations when we are serving our Lord. No matter what the etiquette books say or what our family members tell us is the right thing for us, when we know and love Jesus, all those things are no longer important. She asked us to do what our hearts lead us to do because of the love we feel for Jesus and because of his love for us.

   • Has there been a time in your life when you moved beyond cultural expectations?
   • Have people you loved inadvertently tried to keep you from following your God-given path in the name of their love for you?
   • What does your love of Jesus feel like for you? How does it affect your everyday living?
   • What does Jesus's love for you mean to you?

2. Joanna said to be willing to leave our comfort and security when Jesus calls.

   • Do you relate other stories from the Bible to the call of God to leave one way of being for another way?
   • What are the challenges of leaving what is familiar?
   • What are the blessings of leaving what is familiar?

3. Joanna said even when we are not accepted in our role of sharing our faith because of our background—remember the disciples thought she might be a spy—we should do it anyway.

   • Have you ever not been accepted when you've shared your faith with someone?
   • Have you ever chosen not to share your faith because you feared the other person's reaction?

4. Joanna urged us to consider that when the future seems unknown as it did to her after Jesus's murder, we should trust in the Lord that our path will unfold according to God's plan.

   • Do you have an example of this in your own life?

+ How do you prepare to trust in the Lord that your path will unfold according to God's plan?

5. Joanna said, "Remember that whatever your life journey and circumstances, those particular experiences are exactly what make you unique in God's plan for the world. Embrace your history as you live into God's future."

+ What experiences, both pleasant and unpleasant, have prepared you for who you are today?
+ With the advantage of hindsight, can you now be grateful for painful past experiences because of their lessons for you?
+ Do any of Joanna's calls challenge you in your own life or community? If so, how?
+ Does Joanna's journey stir up a story for you? If so, what?
+ What did you learn from listening to Joanna?
+ Does Joanna's story inspire you to action? If so, what? When? How? Why?

Chapter Four

Mrs. Naaman's Slave Girl—
Compassion and Risk Taking

II Kings 5:1–27

The slave girl of Naaman's wife informed her about the prophet Elisha, who was able to cure Naaman of leprosy.

Early in my career, I was privileged to lead Bible studies and interact with students at a local university. Walking with them in their joys and sorrows was a true blessing to me. I appreciated their trust as I listened to the students struggle with career choices, the changes happening in their lives, and their faith.

I like interacting with and learning from college students. I continue to be blessed as I supervise college and seminary interns when they work with issues of poverty. Sometimes the experience solidifies the students' intent to work in social justice areas when they graduate. For others, the internship helps them discern that their calling lies elsewhere. I enjoy getting to know the young adults and appreciate when our relationships continue past their internships.

Occasionally I interact with other young people who trust me with their struggles to deal with the results of bad decisions, to discern a direction for their lives, and to figure out how to choose healthy friends and relationships. I appreciate the honest conversations we share. I am honored by their trust in me as they share their grief and their dreams.

My relationships with young adults enrich my life more than they will ever know. They teach me in ways that are remarkable to me.

One of my former interns called me to catch up. That led me to think about other students I've engaged with throughout the years. As I sat on the porch, I wondered what had happened to some of them. Specific individuals came to mind—even those I had not thought of in years. Faces floated on the breeze blowing on the porch.

As I was remembering, I looked over and saw a young girl sitting in the chair beside me. She appeared to be in her middle to late teens. I did not remember having someone so young come to visit me. She seemed to be uncomfortable and as unsure of what was going on as I had been the first few times women visited me on the porch. I smiled at her and said, "Welcome. I am glad that you joined me here on my porch."

She replied, "What's going on? I do not understand why I am here or even how I got here."

I explained, "I don't know either how you got here, but I can tell you that a lot of women have sat in the chair where you are now sitting, women from the Bible. When they show up, they share their stories with me. Their experiences help me and other people as we grow in our own lives and our faith. I suspect that you have such a story to share with me. I want to learn from you."

She said, "Well, I don't know about that. I'm just a slave girl."

I was astonished and said, "Really? Who's your mistress or master?"

She replied, "I belong to Naaman, a commander in the army of the king of Aram, but I serve his wife."

I smiled at her, hoping to put her at ease, and said, "Please tell me more about yourself."

Hesitantly at first and then with more boldness, she began. "I am an Israelite. I was taken as a slave during one of the many skirmishes that seem to always be happening between my country and Aram—also called Syria. Both of my older siblings were also enslaved. I do not know what happened to them. I was very fortunate to have ended up with Commander and Mrs. Naaman. Mrs. Naaman treats me almost as a daughter. I like her very much. If I have to be a slave, this is a good place to be. I eat well, and Mrs. Naaman appreciates my work.

"The commander is a very great man. He has status and power. He is well thought of in high circles even though he has leprosy. If he had lived in my home country rather than Syria, he would have been doomed to be cast away so as not to contaminate others. And yet here in this strange culture he is accepted by his own people. I have pondered how it can be that a person can be accepted in one culture and ostracized in another. I like Commander Naaman, and if I had not been taken captive, I would never have been able to know how nice he is. At home, I could not have talked with him or known him.

"However, even with leprosy, Commander Naaman was allowed to do his work. Nevertheless, he still suffered. It hurt my heart to see how he ached with the terrible disease. People stared at him because of the way he looked. Some of them could not see the man for seeing the ravages of the leprosy. Mrs. Naaman would share with me her own pain when she looked at what her husband had to endure. As I brushed my mistress's hair, Mrs. Naaman would muse about her husband's health or lack of it. She was especially distraught one day. In an effort to calm her down and soothe her spirits, I said, 'If only my lord were with the prophet who is in Samaria! He would cure him of his leprosy' (II Kings 5:3).

"I discovered that Mrs. Naaman, as any good wife would, shared with her husband a way for him to be cured. After learning of this possibility for health, the commander went to his boss, the king, and told him what he had learned about the prophet in Samaria. Fortunately the king was enlightened and cared for his employee and encouraged the commander to do whatever it took to get well. The king even paid for the treatment and sent his personal request for assistance to the king of Israel. Are there bosses in your time who do these kind things?

"What I tell you next is only what I heard. One of my friends in the household is the daughter of one of the commander's servants. Her father accompanied the commander on his trip to Israel. My friend told me that first the group went directly to the king of Israel. I suppose this is the proper protocol for military men and politicians. The commander took a letter from his king along with all kinds of treasures: silver, gold, and beautiful clothing. He gave the letter and the wonderful gifts to the king of Israel.

However, the Israelite king misinterpreted what the commander was doing. I found out that he tore his clothes in fear and grief and said, 'Am I God, to give death or life, that this man sends word to me to cure a man of leprosy? Just look and see how he is trying to pick a quarrel with me' (II Kings 5:7). I told you that in my country, leprosy is treated very poorly! Can you imagine what the king of Israel must have felt?"

I replied that I thought I could. Then I began smiling. At first she reacted as if I had insulted her. When I realized that she did not know what I was thinking, I said, "I do not mean to make light of what you are saying. I am smiling because I was imagining how that kind of thing would be handled today. Almost immediately it would be on CNN or Twitter with the sound bite, 'King of Aram challenges king of Israel. Our king has been placed in a no-win situation. The king grievously announces that war is imminent.'"

I knew that she had no idea what CNN or Twitter were, but she was trained to be polite. My young friend nodded and demonstrated her insight when she said, "It is a good thing that the king of my homeland, Israel, knew that only our holy God heals. That shows my king's wisdom and understanding about following our God."

She explained further, "Commander Naaman would have made him uncomfortable because of the leprosy. If the king touched anything that the commander had touched, the king would become unclean."

I nodded my understanding, and she continued. "He must have put on quite a distressing show, because Elisha, the man of God I had told Mrs. Naaman about, heard of the king's torment. Elisha sent a message to the king. 'Why have you torn your clothes? Let him come to me, that he may learn that there is a prophet in Israel' (II Kings 5:8).

"So the king sent Naaman and his entourage to Elisha's house. I imagine that it was quite a sight to behold: chariots, horses, wagons filled with gifts, and people in the traveling party who were clothed in different styles of dress. I would have run out the door just to see the parade, but that is not what Elisha did. He sent a messenger out of the house to say, 'Go, wash in the Jordan seven times, and your flesh shall be restored and you shall be clean' (II Kings 5:10)."

The girl looked at me with raised eyebrows to note my reaction. I guess that I looked amazed at this point in her story. I commented, "If I had just driven miles and miles to a famous hospital and was told by a receptionist to go across the street and eat a hamburger at a fast-food restaurant and I would be healed, I would not have reacted well. I would have expected to give my medical history and records to several health-care professionals and then have to endure many diagnostic tests. When I have major illnesses, major problems, or major setbacks, I expect major cure processes."

She replied, "And Commander Naaman was the same. He got angry that he had been told to take a bath in a puny little river. If bathing was all it took, goodness knows, there were larger rivers in his homeland where he could have bathed. He thought that Elisha would at least come out and pray loudly and wave his hand to cure the leprosy. Probably Elisha could have done that, but if he had, who would have gotten the credit for the cure? God? Probably not. Elisha? Most certainly."

She paused in her story to ask thoughtfully, "Have you ever prayed to God for something, for a change to occur or for a miracle to happen, and had in mind how you expected that to happen? I know I have. When I was first captured, I poured out my heart and wept, calling out to God to release me from my fate. I guess I was like Commander Naaman. As I've grown, I can now think of lots of times when my prayers have been answered … just not in the way I anticipated. Being with Mrs. Naaman was certainly an answer to one of my prayers. She is such a wonderful woman to me. I feel loved and cared for even though I am a mere slave."

I interjected, "I once heard a sermon where the preacher declared that God always answers prayer. Sometimes the answer is yes, sometimes it is no, sometimes it is not yet, and sometimes it is maybe. My experience says that preacher was right."

We rocked together, thinking our individual thoughts. I assumed we were both thinking of prayers that had been answered in various ways in our lives. Then I asked, "What happened next?"

She said, "My friend told me that her father saved the day when he said to the commander, 'Father, if the prophet had commanded you to do something difficult, would you not have done it? How much more, when

31

all he said to you was, 'Wash and be clean?' (II Kings 5:13). My friend said that she heard her father ask her mother, 'What if I had followed the human codes which said that slaves do not confront their masters? What if I believed that the master was always right, no matter what? What if I had been scared to state the obvious?'"

The young woman continued, "I think these are good questions for all of us to consider. Do we sometimes remain quiet because we believe that is the proper thing to do? Are there times when we might speak up for the good of another, even when doing so may be risky?"

She paused again as if letting her questions soak in to her and to me. I was amazed at the maturity and wisdom of this young woman. I waited until she was ready to continue her story.

She said, "Well, Commander Naaman did go wash seven times in the Jordan and was healed. He wasn't just healed. He was powerfully healed. His flesh became like that of a young boy. The commander proclaimed to everyone around, 'Now I know that there is no other God in all the earth except in Israel' (II Kings 5:15). Mrs. Naaman told me later that her husband knew that his life had been transformed in more ways that just having his body healed of the leprosy.

"But my story does not end there. The commander's confession was followed by a dose of reality because he knew that he would return to serve his king. The commander was concerned about what he should do when the king went to worship at the temple of Rimmon, because the king always leaned on the arm of Commander Naaman. He knew that when the king bowed down, he would have to bow down as well. Because the commander had just professed faith in the one and only God, the God of Israel, he was concerned about how to continue to serve his king as a public servant while serving the holy Lord of Israel.

"When my friend told me this part of what she'd heard her father tell her mother, I too was stumped about how to handle this dilemma. It turns out that Elisha told him he could go through the motions of bowing down and to go in peace. Isn't this remarkable? Our God understands that sometimes actions and deep beliefs have to be compromised a bit. I'm amazed!"

I replied, "Yes, I'm amazed too. I wish I had Elisha around sometimes to help me figure out those kinds of things. I'd love to have him tell me to go in peace."

"Mrs. Naaman later told me that her husband did ask for something that would signify his newfound faith in the God of Israel, the one God. He asked to take two mule loads of earth with him. She explained to me, her lowly servant girl, that this was more than a souvenir of his journey. By taking some of the soil from Israel, the commander was taking the homeland of the God of Israel with him so he could continue to worship this awesome God. If he had not taken some of the land of Israel with him, the commander was afraid that the God of Israel would not come with him. The dirt helped him to connect with his newfound faith.

"My story helps me understand the profound reality of God's inclusive love and grace. My story shows me that none of us should categorize people into our own definitions of what may be right or wrong. For God, there is no us and them. Commander Naaman, an outsider to the faith of Israel, was provided health and healing for both physical and spiritual ills. And do you know what? People do not like hearing this!"

I was aware of her innocent and profound insights. I remembered the story in the Gospel of Luke when Jesus preached a sermon in his hometown, Nazareth. He said, point blank, "There were many lepers in Israel in the time of the prophet Elisha, and none of them was cleansed except Naaman the Syrian" (Luke 4:27). This was the last comment Jesus made before the congregation became enraged and drove Jesus out of the town with the intent to kill him.

why?

My young friend finished her story with these words, "As I think about it, there were a lot of players in this story of God's love for all of us. There was me, a slave girl; Mrs. Naaman, who deeply loved and cared for her husband; the king of Syria; the king of Israel; the commander's servant; and Elisha. If any one of us had kept silent, God's impact on the commander's life could have been so different. It's wonderful, isn't it, that something as insignificant as my comment to Mrs. Naaman could have ended in such a glorious way! It just goes to show that God works in amazing ways, even with me, a slave girl. I never dreamed I would be remembered all these centuries. I simply shared my beliefs with compassion while I went about my everyday chores. I guess I ask you to think about whether there are opportunities for you to share with compassion your beliefs as you go about your everyday life. Are there insignificant people like me, an unnamed slave girl, to whom you should be listening?"

I looked at her with tears in my eyes. I marveled that out of such youth came such a powerful testimony. I told her, "You humbled me in profound ways. You did not judge. You simply told me your story and what you thought. You are a truly remarkable young woman and messenger from God."

She bowed her head and left me.

Reflecting on the Slave Girl's Visit

1. The girl said that she had pondered how it can be that a person can be accepted in one culture and ostracized in another.

    •   Do you know any immigrants? What is their experience of being ostracized?

    •   Have you ever felt like you were a stranger in a new situation? How did you handle this? What kinds of behaviors did you feel you had to change?

2. The girl said that the king even paid for the treatment and sent his personal request for assistance to the king of Israel. She asked if there are bosses in our time who do these kind things.

    •   How would you answer her question?

3. The girl asked, "Have you ever prayed to God for something, for a change to occur or a miracle to happen, and had in mind how you expected that to happen?" She went on to say, "I can now think of lots of times when my prayers have been answered ... just not in the way I anticipated."

    •   When you pray, do you already have the solution in mind? Do you know how you want God to endorse your request?

+ What are the challenges to you for praying and leaving the answer totally to God?

4. The girl asked, "Do we sometimes remain quiet because we believe that is the proper thing to do? Are there times when we might speak up for the good of another, even when doing so may be risky?"

   + Have you ever kept quiet when you felt that you should have spoken? What stopped you?
   + Who in your community might need you to speak up?
   + How might you be an advocate for someone or some issue that needs addressing?

5. The girl said that her story helped her understand the profound reality of God's inclusive love and grace. Her story showed her that none of us should categorize people into our own definitions of what may be right or wrong. For God, there is not us and them.

   + How do you respond to this comment?
   + Does her story inspire you to action? If so, what? When? How? Why?

6. The girl asked us to think about whether there are opportunities for us to share with compassion our beliefs as we go about our everyday lives. Are there insignificant people like this unnamed slave girl to whom we should be listening? *yes!*

   + How do you respond to her question?
   + Does the girl challenge you in your own life or community? If so, how?
   + Does her journey stir up a story for you? If so, what?
   + What did you learn from listening to the slave girl?

Chapter Five

Priscilla—Using Your Gifts

Acts 18:1–4, 18–21, 24–28; Romans 16:3; I Cor.16:19; II Tim.4:19

Priscilla, along with her husband, Aquila, helped Paul spread the gospel of Jesus Christ throughout the Roman Empire.

I am regularly surprised when the opportunity comes to me to share my understanding of the gospel of Jesus Christ. I don't mean in a church setting. I'm talking about during my usual daily meanderings. I may be conversing with someone about ordinary happenings, and before I realize it, we begin talking about what faith means or what walking in Jesus's way looks and feels like. These spontaneous conversations are much more real or profound than any sermon I have ever preached. I am always grateful that God placed me at the right place at the right time. I learn as much from what pops out of my mouth as the other person does—probably more.

It was the end of such a day. I was relaxing on the porch in that sweet time between the end of the work day and the beginning of an evening with my husband. I looked over and saw a very aristocratic-looking woman sitting in the chair beside me. I was a little embarrassed at the shabby appearance of the porch. I hoped that the loose webbing on the rocking chair did not snag her gown.

I said, "Welcome to this porch. What is your name?"

She looked at me warmly with kind and soft eyes. She said, "My name is Priscilla."

I wanted to make sure that she was the person I thought she was. I asked, "Is your husband's name Aquila, and did you both work with Paul?"

She smiled gently and nodded.

"I am so glad that you have come to visit with me. I want to hear about your house church, your travels, and what Paul was really like."

At that she laughed. "I will tell you some of what you want to know. I will not speak very much about Paul, since you can already know what you need to learn about him by reading his letters. His epistles are full of his testimony, which is what is most important about him."

I think my face must have registered my disappointment, because Priscilla said, "I have plenty to tell you without taking my time to tell you about Paul."

I realized my rudeness and replied, "Dear lady, of course you are correct. Please tell me your story and share with me your wisdom."

Priscilla began. "I grew up in Rome in a very privileged environment. My family was nobility. I never lacked for anything. We were surrounded by slaves, merchants, and tradespeople. Many of the wonders of the world came into our household: luscious foods, beautiful fabrics, exotic glassware, and an exuberance of ideas. I was loved. My parents offered me opportunities to learn about the world that most people, especially women, did not have. We traveled beyond Rome, so I was comfortable thinking of myself as a citizen of the world.

"Because I had relative freedom in the household, I was able to interact with all the people who worked and visited there. One day I noticed a strikingly handsome young man who was repairing some of our awnings. Because the sun was hot that day, I offered him some pomegranate juice. He was focused on his work and had not seen me coming toward him. When my offer of a refreshing beverage finally registered with him, he looked up from the canvas. I saw the startled expression in his eyes that quickly turned to deep appreciation. I don't know if you believe in the idea of loving someone from the first minute you see that person, but that is what happened between Aquila and me.

"We began chatting while he worked. We tried not to draw attention to ourselves, because he needed this massive job that my father had given to him and I did not want to be forbidden to talk with him. As the days progressed, our love for each other deepened.

"Finally we decided that we had to approach my parents and ask for permission to marry. They liked Aquila and appreciated his work, but they were not happy. It was not right that a nobleman's daughter should marry a skilled laborer. I begged and begged.

"My father asked me how I supposed I would be able to live as I had been brought up. I was accustomed to luxury. What could Aquila provide for me?

"My youth and my love for Aquila gave me the answer. I retorted, 'I'll learn to be a tentmaker too!'

"My father scoffed and asked, 'You will ruin your beautiful hands by sewing the tents?'

"You know what I answered. I said, 'Yes, Father.'

"With that, my parents realized that I was not going to be talked out of marrying Aquila. They gave me their blessing, provided that we remain in their household. At the time, neither of us saw a problem with that. By day I worked alongside my husband learning his trade. By night … well, I'll not talk about that.

"But then Claudius changed our lives. He ordered all of us Jews to leave Rome. He was afraid of our power and especially of the Christians. He thought the Christians were a sect of Judaism, but of course that was not true. However, Jews and Christians were all the same to him.

"My parents decided that Corinth would be a good place to move to. It was a cosmopolitan commercial center. Along with my parents, Aquila and I packed up and left my childhood home to go to Corinth. We knew that the city was large enough to offer plenty of work for accomplished tentmakers. Aquila and I settled in there and began to develop a reputation for the quality of our work.

"Our lives changed once again when an itinerant tentmaker, new to Corinth, came to us seeking work. His name was Paul. Yes, *that* Paul. He stayed with us, and while we worked together, he talked about what had happened to him on the way to Damascus and about Jesus. Paul had been an extremely devout Jew, and now he was a devout apostle of Jesus committed to spreading the good news throughout the gentile world. Because of Paul, Aquila and I became Christians. We began sharing in Paul's ministry during his year and a half in Corinth. The church at Corinth met in our home.

"When Paul left Corinth, Aquila and I went with him. We wanted to be part of this wondrous message of love, shalom, peace, and community. We preached our way to Syria and then to Ephesus. While we were there, a man named Apollos began preaching the gospel of Jesus Christ, but he was not fully knowledgeable about the way of Jesus. His message was based more on John's proclamation. Apollos was a dynamic preacher—eloquent and knowledgeable about the scriptures. Aquila and I knew that he could be a powerful missionary and preacher of the gospel if he had just a little guidance. So we took him aside and mentored him. We corrected some of his misconceptions and helped him clarify his message of Jesus's way.

"Paul got into serious trouble with the local authorities. As you know, he was very good at doing that. Because of my Roman citizenship, Aquila and I intervened on his behalf. Paul later credited us with saving his life when he wrote his letter to our church in Rome: 'Greet Prisca and Aquila, who work with me in Christ Jesus, and who risked their necks for my life' (Romans 16:3). I don't know that I would categorize our actions to that extreme. We were just glad to ensure that Paul could continue his important missionary work.

"When we eventually returned to Rome, we moved back into my family home. Because we had a large dining space, unlike most of the people who lived in Rome, we invited the Christian community to meet in our house. Indeed, our whole household was baptized into the gospel of Jesus Christ. I remember especially the young gentile girl Nesta who our main gardener had found abandoned and exposed at the edge of our garbage heap. He brought the pitiful thing in, and we fed and nurtured her. As soon as she was old enough, we baptized her. She eventually became my personal slave. She and I would pray together and share the joy of our lives in Christ while she brushed my hair or helped me dress.

"Our household manager, Aurelia, was a gentile. She learned to cook and keep house in the manner that our Jewish background preferred. She, as a member of our household, was baptized as well. She had been challenged enough by maintaining the household with all the comings and goings of the tradespeople and my own work. When peasants, skilled laborers, educated and uneducated people, and slaves began coming to our home for regular worship, she really was not happy. She would mutter, 'Those people come because life is better for them here than outside. They just want something to eat. They can think they are somebody. Humph!' She did not realize how nearly she spoke the truth.

"Christianity did offer people opportunities that no other group in Rome did. The mystery religions and even the trades communities required initiation fees that many people could not afford. Christianity gave voice and position to women—which was rare in Rome. But the gospel of love and mutual caring for one another was indeed good news for us all. As Paul taught, 'There is no longer Jew or Greek, there is no longer slave or free, there is no longer male and female; for all of you are one in Christ Jesus' (Galatians 3:28). This is the gospel we shared, and people were hungry for such good news.

"Paul eventually came to Rome but as a prisoner. However, he was able to maintain communication with us and others with whom he had worked. He prayed constantly for all the churches he had established on his journeys. We visited with him regularly so we could feed each other spiritually. We always brought him tasty morsels that Aurelia prepared especially for him. For some reason, she liked him even though she barely tolerated some of the people who were part of our household church. God does work in mysterious ways!

"I'll end my story here. Whatever happened next is not important in the triumph of the gospel that Paul, Aquila, and I were able to share. However, I learned a number of things as I traveled this journey. The first is that God can turn your life upside down. I was born to nobility but chose to leave that life. I never regretted my marriage to Aquila or our lives together as missionaries and tentmakers. When God offers an opportunity, embrace the challenges and joys of your new direction.

"The second is to help people realize how they benefit from the color of their skin, their speech patterns, or their knowledge of social expectations—whether they know it or not. I was not born a peasant, but I could mingle with all kinds of people because of the love of Jesus Christ that I knew. I could provide some physical comfort through my hospitality of home and food. Doors opened to me not because of who I was but because of my

[handwritten: your worth is by who you belong to — decided]

citizenship and noble birth. My background allowed us to rescue Paul from certain death and also afforded a place for our Christian brothers and sisters to meet. Help people understand that their privilege is not to be taken for granted and they need to realize the benefits they enjoy are through no effort on their own. Encourage them to use their benefits for others. I was born to nobility. I never could assume those benefits were something I had earned myself. I wanted to share my blessings with others.

"The third lesson is what I gained from my housekeeper, Aurelia. I know that people decide not to reach out to help others because they do not agree with life choices, life circumstances, or behaviors. Aurelia judged the motives of some of the people who came to the church in our house. But the love of Jesus Christ is open to all—to everyone, male, female, Jew, Greek, slave, or free. Hospitality is an honor when one serves God. Even Aurelia decided that she wanted to minister to Paul. Who could have guessed that would happen?

"And finally, share the gospel wherever you can in whatever circumstances you find yourself. If you need some help with that as Apollos did, then seek out someone to guide or mentor you. But share what you know. You know the love of Christ. Share that with others. You may not have to speak words. You can exhibit the good news by how you live, how you interact with others, what you value, and who you spend time with.

"I had a full and rich life. It was certainly not the life I thought would be mine when I was just a young girl. It was so much more than I could ever have imagined. For that, all I can say is praise be to God."

She had delivered her message to me and left immediately.

[handwritten: Well-known minister]

Reflecting on Priscilla's Visit

1. Priscilla said that God can turn your life upside down. When God offers an opportunity, embrace the challenges and joys of your new direction.

   • What is your response to this observation? Has this ever happened to you?

   • When you have a hint that your life is about to take a new direction, are you more likely to embrace it with joy or with anxiety? Why?

2. Priscilla charged us to help people realize how they benefit from the color of their skin, their speech patterns, or their knowledge of social expectations. Help people understand that their privilege is not to be taken for granted and they need to realize the benefits they enjoy are through no effort on their own. Encourage them to use their benefits for others.

   + In what ways are you privileged?
   + How can you use your privileges and talents for the glory of God and the benefit of others?

3. Priscilla knows that people decide not to reach out to help others because they do not agree with life choices, life circumstances, or behaviors. But the love of Jesus Christ is open to all—to everyone, male, female, Jew, Greek, slave, or free. Hospitality is an honor when one serves God.

   + How are you challenged by Priscilla's observation?
   + Are there people in your circle of friends and acquaintances who are different from you? If not, do you want to expand your social circle? If you do, how might you begin?

4. Priscilla told us to share the gospel wherever we can in whatever circumstances we find ourselves. If we need help with that as Apollos did, then we should seek out someone to guide or mentor us. She urges us to share what we know.

   + Who have been your mentors?
   + Whom might you become a mentor to?

5. Priscilla said, "You know the love of Christ. Share that with others. You may not have to speak words. You can exhibit the good news by how you live, how you interact with others, what you value, and who you spend time with."

   + In what ways can you share the love of Christ without words?
   + Do any of Priscilla's calls challenge you in your own life or community? If so, how?

Priscilla may have written Hebrews according to research + scholars –

- Does her journey stir up a story for you? If so, what?
- What did you learn from listening to Priscilla?
- Does her story inspire you to action? If so, what? When? How? Why?

Chapter Six

Queen of Sheba—Curiosity and Living Fully

544   699
I Kings 10:1–13; II Chronicles 9:1-12

The Queen of Sheba visited Solomon and brought him fine gifts. She returned to Sheba with all she had asked.

Recent negotiations over a distressing situation had been particularly difficult. I thought I knew and understood what the other people wanted. I knew what I intended to obtain in the agreement. I was fairly clear in my mind what my alternative or number two position would be. I was solid about what I absolutely would not do or agree to. In other words, I was as prepared as I could be.

What I had not counted on was that the other people were not clear at all about what outcome they were seeking. One person said one thing and another said something else. Several were operating with false information as well as what others had told them.

Our discussions became more and more heated. Trust disappeared, and bad feelings made keeping a calm demeanor difficult. There was a point when it appeared that one or more people would leave the room in anger rather than complete the negotiations.

Finally the meeting ended with a tentative agreement, but I knew that we were not close to a final decision. I suspected that some of us would feel like winners while others felt like losers. I went to the porch when I got home to soothe my wounded spirit.

As I rocked, I went over and over the conversations. I fumed about what that person said and what another party implied. I wished I had said something differently. I was exhausted and knew that on another day, we'd go at it again. What made the situation particularly painful is that I'm trained in conflict resolution and have helped groups negotiate their way through turmoil. Yet here I was, embroiled in a conflict, and I felt powerless. I realized that I was skilled in conflict management and negotiating when I was not directly involved. However, when I was caught in the middle of something, I could not be dispassionate about the outcome.

I kept playing the "if only" and "what if" games in my mind. I realized that I was rocking faster and faster as my anger began to rise. I closed my eyes and blew out a big breath of air as if in resignation. I tried then to breathe deeply and to let the porch's calm seep into my soul. With my eyes closed, I began to hear the early evening birds calling to each other. The rate of my rocking began to slow.

I finally opened my eyes and was surprised to see that someone was sitting in the other rocking chair. I had been so absorbed in my own issues that I had not realized I had company. The woman was beautiful and commanded attention. She was very regal. Since I did not know when she had shown up, I was embarrassed that she might have seen me so agitated.

I tried to compose myself even more and put on what I'm sure looked like a fake smile and said, "Welcome. Will you please tell me who you are?"

She replied, "I am the Queen of Sheba."

My curiosity heightened, and I began to let go of my brooding. Here was, after all, the Queen of Sheba! I genuinely smiled and greeted her, "Hello, Your Majesty. I'm glad that you are here. I want to hear your story and learn what you have to teach me."

She nodded her head toward me and said, "That's why I am here."

I waited for her to begin, but she just sat there very composed. I bit my lower lip and wondered how to proceed. Then I realized I was curious about something. I said, "Your Majesty, I have a question. Where is Sheba?"

She responded, "Sheba no longer exists, since that was more than three thousand years ago, in the tenth century BCE. I have heard that my kingdom was part of what is known today as Yemen and Ethiopia."

I thought she was so beautiful, but she was also a woman of power. I asked another question. "Was it usual in your time and place for women to have the kinds of power and riches that you had?"

The queen smiled slightly and said, "I can understand why you may think that my role as queen was rare, because you do not read about such powerful female rulers in your scriptures. However, it is true that strong women rulers were present in Egypt and Arabia in the time before and after my story."

I realized that I had controlled the conversation with my questions and not allowed her to tell her story. I said, "Please forgive me, Your Majesty. I've been busy asking questions and have not allowed you to speak with me as you wish."

"Oh, you do not need my forgiveness. I too am a woman of curiosity. After all, that's why I visited King Solomon. I wanted to see for myself this man of wisdom whom I had heard so much about. His reputation was that he was a follower of the Lord of Israel, wealthy, and very wise. I decided to visit him. Of course, I also wanted to work out some trade agreements between his country and mine for our mutual benefit.

"I instructed my people to load up our caravan with spices, gold, and precious stones. We traveled about twelve hundred miles so I could make this political alliance as well as discover if the man was as great as he was reported to be. The journey was long and arduous. We had a large caravan and moved slowly. We also needed to watch for bandits or thieves because we were transporting so many riches.

"I believe that other rulers may have sent their ambassadors to Solomon's court, but I wanted to make the journey myself. The commercial aspects of our alliance were too important for me to trust the task to anyone else. This is something that I hope you pay attention to. When something is extremely important for you and people you are responsible for, address the issue directly yourself. Do not entrust your passion and plan to someone else. There were times along the journey when I wished that I had decided to stay in Sheba and had sent someone else in my place, but the stakes were too high. I was the one who needed to do all the negotiations. No one else. Remember that even though the journey was very hard, wonderful things happened for me and my kingdom.

"I wanted my gifts to be significant to the great King Solomon. All totaled, the spices, jewels, and gold were equal to about 15 to 18 percent of the king's wealth. I figured that if my mission were successful, we would more than compensate Sheba for the value of our gifts. I knew that I needed to get the king's attention. I had traveled too far to chance being ignored. I encourage you to plan well when you have big dreams and aspirations. Be generous with your gifts, and your generosity will come back to you. You may not have gold and jewels to give. However, you can give your time and presence. I know that King Solomon was impressed with my personal visit, which may have been more important to him than all the finery. I am convinced that my willingness to come to King Solomon was instrumental in our political liaison and eventual trade agreements.

"When I and my caravan entered Jerusalem, we made quite a picture—camels and more camels laden with packs that were richly decorated with jewels and golden threads. Trumpeters blew horns, children danced around our feet, and people stopped in the streets and stared. I had come to make a statement, and we certainly did that!

"When King Solomon learned of our arrival, he sent for me. I let out a big breath, never realizing that I had been holding it while waiting to learn the king's reaction to our presence. I adorned myself with my finest robes and went to see him.

"I told the king that I had heard of his wisdom and wanted to see for myself if the stories were true. He asked me what I had heard. I told him of the time when the two prostitutes both claimed the same baby as their own. Both women had given birth about the same time. The child of one woman died in the night, so she switched the babies, claiming the live one as her own. The women were brought before Solomon for him to settle their grievances. I repeated the words that Solomon had spoken. I said, 'You told your guard in front of the women to bring you a sword so you could divide the living boy in two. Then you said, "Give half to the one, and half to the other"' (I Kings 3:24–25). The real mother said to give her son to the other woman. She did not want her child to be murdered.

"I watched the king's eyes the entire time I was telling the story. Even though his face was impassive, his eyes lit up when I began the story. When I finished, he said, 'You have heard well. Now let us talk.'

"The details of our conversation remain confidential. I asked many questions and even some riddles to test his knowledge and wisdom. He answered every one. We spent many hours over several weeks talking and learning each other's strengths and weaknesses. We began to negotiate how our two kingdoms would support and help each other. We each had resources that the other needed.

"While I was in the palace for our deliberations, I was impressed with all the wealth I saw. His house was beautiful beyond description. His government officials were well trained and knowledgeable. Even his servants were dressed in lovely garments. And the sacrifices to his God? Oh my, they were offered continuously, or that's how it seemed to me. I knew that we were equals in our negotiations.

"We continued our conversations. I knew enough about the vanity of a king to give him compliments ... which were true, of course, but still given to bolster our strategies for trade. I told the king, 'The report was true that I heard in my own land of your accomplishments and of your wisdom, but I did not believe the reports until I came and my own eyes had seen it. Not even half had been told me; your wisdom and prosperity far surpass the report that I had heard. Happy are your wives! Happy are these your servants, who continually attend you and hear your wisdom!' (I Kings 10: 6–8).

"The king was still a man, and I could see him trying not to puff himself up. I truly did admire him. My words were not lies. I just embellished them a bit for effect. Then I added, 'Blessed be the Lord your God, who has delighted in you and set you on the throne of Israel! Because the Lord loved Israel forever, he has made you king to execute justice and righteousness' (I Kings 10:9).

"King Solomon agreed to every one of my requests for Sheba. I gave him all the gifts that we had brought to him. He, in turn, gave me beautiful gifts to carry back to Sheba. I was extremely satisfied with our visit and the political gains we had agreed upon. We left with everything and more than I had hoped for and had an uneventful trip back to Sheba."

I looked at my guest with tremendous admiration. I said, "That's an inspiring story, especially since it seems you negotiated as an equal ruler— almost, dare I say, man-to-man? You are truly remarkable."

The queen rocked and even smirked a little when I complimented her. I suppose that Solomon was not the only monarch who liked compliments.

Then I asked, "May I ask you another question?"

She said, "Of course. You should know by now that I appreciate questions."

"What you've told me is basically what is in the Old Testament story of your interaction with King Solomon. However, there are other stories or legends about what happened next. Some people believe that you and Solomon were physically intimate and that you had a son who became the king of Abyssinia. Others tell of your conversion to Islam. I've seen paintings where you were one sexy woman. Movies have been made of your interaction with Solomon. There was one where Gina Lollobrigida played you and Tyrone Power played Solomon. That was steamy. Is any of that true?"

Then I saw the queen pull herself up with all the regal posture that was possible. She looked me in the eye. I thought, *Okay, now I'm going to find out what really happened, and I can tell the world.* She smiled. Then she settled back down into the rocking chair and rocked, and rocked, and rocked.

I began to relax back into my chair and follow the rhythm of her back-and-forth movements. I waited.

Finally, the queen said, "Do you remember that I told you the details of the conversation between King Solomon and me remained confidential?"

I nodded.

She said, "There is your answer."

I must have looked disappointed, because she said, "I charge you to live your life to the fullest that you possibly can. Use everything at your disposal to take care of yourself and those who depend on you. Most importantly, never care what other people think or say about you. You know your truth. What others believe about you is really none of your business."

I was gently chastised by the beautiful and gracious queen. When she saw that I had absorbed her words, she left. I think I heard the faint tinkling of camel bells in the distance.

Reflecting on the Queen of Sheba's Visit

1. The queen said that when something is extremely important for you and people you are responsible for, address the issue directly yourself. Do not entrust your passion and plan to someone else.

   + What is your response to this directive?
   + On the other hand, are there times when others could very capably handle something and you have trouble letting go? If so, is there anything you can learn from the queen?

2. The queen asked us to remember that even though the journey was very hard, wonderful things happened for her and her kingdom.

   + Have you ever gotten through a difficult situation and then realized that you were extremely happy with the eventual outcome?
   + When you were in the middle of a difficult phase of your life, did your faith sustain you? If so, how? If not, what helped you continue through the process?

3. The queen encouraged us to plan well when we have big dreams and aspirations. We are to be generous with our gifts, and our generosity will come back to us.

   + How do you plan? Do you plan alone, or do you invite others into your process?
   + Do you believe the statement about being generous and our generosity coming back to us? Why or why not?

4. The queen reminded us that we can give our time and presence.

   + When have you been the recipient of someone's gift of time or presence? How did you feel?
   + What are occasions when gifts of time or presence are particularly helpful or appreciated? *times of crisis, illness; when feeling down; unexpected*

5. The queen reminded us to live life to the fullest and to use everything at our disposal to take care of ourselves and those who depend on us.

    ✦ When do you live your life to the fullest? What kinds of things hinder this kind of living?
    ✦ When you have lived small, what were your fears and challenges?
    ✦ How would you help someone figure out how to live fully?

6. The Queen of Sheba said never to care what other people think or say about you. She reminded us that we know our truth and that what others believe about us is really none of our business.

    ✦ Do you believe this?
    ✦ When others have made you feel less than you know yourself to be, how would the queen's advice have changed your reaction?
    ✦ Do any of the queen's calls challenge you in your own life or community? If so, how?
    ✦ Does her journey stir up a story for you? If so, what?
    ✦ What did you learn from listening to the Queen of Sheba?
    ✦ Does her story inspire you to action? If so, what? When? How? Why?

"No one can make you feel inferior without your permission" Eleanor Roosevelt

Chapter Seven

Rahab—Intrigue, Family, and Fearless Actions

Joshua 2 and 6; Hebrews 11:31; James 2:25; Matthew 1:5

Rahab helped Israelite spies escape from Jericho. For her efforts, she and her family were protected during the siege of Jericho. She is listed in the genealogy of Jesus.

For about three years, I was privileged to work with women who were at least two of these four things: homeless, pregnant, addicts, or working as prostitutes. As I learned more about the lives of these women and we began to know each other as real people, not as program participants and an administrator, I shared stories of our interactions with my own family. I found the women absolutely delightful—for the most part—and wanted my sons to appreciate these women for who they were and not what they did.

One of my favorite stories to share with groups happened because of my relationships with these women. I live in a neighborhood that at one time was very diverse. Our next-door neighbors were first-generation immigrants. In this particular family, the father believed it his duty to introduce his son to a prostitute when he came of age. This young man was chronologically older than my sons but emotionally younger. One day when I came home from work, I asked my sons how their day had been. One of them said, "Do you know what Nate said?" (Nate is not his real name.)

I said, "No, what?"

"He said, 'Let's go downtown and get us a ho.'"

I replied, "Excuse me?"

My son looked exasperated and repeated, "A ho."

I repeated, "What?"

He said, "You know, Mom, a whore!"

My eyes opened wide, and I exclaimed, "What did you tell Nate?"

"I said, 'No way. Our mom knows them all!'"

Then I pause when telling the story and wait for the laughter to explode. I usually raise my arms in the air and grin a hooray kind of smile.

I had told that story at a recent gathering and was smiling to myself as I relaxed on the porch. I was certain that I did not know all the prostitutes in my city, but I was glad that my sons thought I did. I was musing about how privileged I felt to have been invited into the lives of women who often felt they had no options. In our times together, the women learned that their lives could be different. I've kept up with some of them throughout the years. Some have done well and are living healthy and productive lives they are now proud of. Some are dead. Some rode that roller coaster of sobriety followed by an addiction relapse followed by sobriety and then relapse, on and on.

I realized that I had been joined by someone. I had to pull myself back to the present. I greeted the woman. "Hello. I apologize for not immediately acknowledging your presence. I was reminiscing about some wonderful people in my life."

She said, "That's okay. I know I just showed up without warning."

I replied, "I'm used to that by now. What's your name?"

"Rahab."

I thought to myself, *Of course, who else would it be? I've just been thinking about women who were prostitutes. Rahab's visit makes perfect sense!* However, I said, "Welcome to the porch. I'd appreciate your sharing your story and your wisdom with me."

She jumped right into her narrative.

"I don't put up with trivial matters. I just do what has to be done. My family was not able to provide for all our members. Times were hard. War was all around us. The desert wanderers who called themselves Israelites had been attacking various cities in our country. I had to do what needed to be done to protect my relatives. Therefore, I welcomed visitors to my house. And it was my house—make no mistake about that. My house did not belong to any man. It was mine.

"I was able to get my house because it was built onto the wall that surrounded Jericho. Some people did not want houses located on the wall because they did not feel safe. Others looked with raised eyebrows at some of us who lived on the wall because wall dwellers, as they called us, had a certain reputation. Men came to see me. Often they were just looking for a bed for the night. Sometimes they wanted the comfort of a woman. I'm not bragging or confessing. I'm just telling you like it was.

"I also ran a textile business out of my home. I wove fabric out of the flax that I dried on my rooftop. Growing and preparing the flax was hard work, but I had a lot of relatives who needed me. Members of my family helped me with the cloth and running our inn. We worked together in order to feel safe and to thrive. I suspect that you'd do the same thing for your family.

"One day two guys from Shittim came to my house looking for lodging. Because the king of Jericho had men who watched my house regularly to see who was coming and going, he learned that my guests were Israelite spies. I did not know that. In my line of work, I've learned not to ask too many questions. However, I also know how to protect my guests. One of my nephews watched the king's men who watched my house.

"My nephew slipped into the house and told me that our guests were spies sent by the desert wanderers' leader, Joshua. I went to the two men and whispered to them to follow me. I led them to the roof and hid them among the flax that was drying there. I did not want to get into trouble with the king's men for helping these Israelites. I also did not want to get into trouble with Joshua's men if indeed the Israelites were planning to attack Jericho. You see, I had learned the skills of self-preservation early in life.

"In the early evening, just before the city gates were closed so that no one could come in or go out, the king's men banged their fists on my door. I answered their rude knocking with a questioning look on my face as if I had no idea why they were there. When they ordered me to bring out the two men who were staying with me, I put on my most innocent expression and said, 'True, the men came to me, but I did not know where they came from.

55

And when it was time to close the gate at dark, the men went out. Where the men went I do not know. Pursue them quickly, for you can overtake them' (Joshua 2:4–5).

"Rather than search my house, the king's men decided it was prudent to get out of the city before the gates were closed so they could capture the Israelite spies. They left without searching my home. I took a deep breath and sat down to decide what my next steps would be. I still had the two men, whom the king's men had confirmed as Israelite spies, on my roof. Remember, I do what I have to do to take care of my family. I meditated on my next steps. Then I had my plan.

"I went to the roof and told the men they could come out. I told them I knew they were spies sent by their leader, Joshua. I said that I'd heard about their battles and how they'd conquered other cities and killed many, if not all, of the inhabitants. I mentioned the stories some of my guests had told about the Red Sea escape and the total destruction of Sihon and Og.

"The men confirmed everything I told them. With my heart pounding, I then acknowledged that I and my family were frightened of them and what they were planning to do to us. But remember, I know how to take care of myself and my family. I added, 'The Lord your God is indeed God in heaven above and on earth below' (Joshua 2:11). Honestly, I was not sure if I believed that statement, but I figured that it could not hurt since it seemed that the Israelites believed they were fighting a holy war to claim the land that their God had given to them. At this point, I decided to cast my future with the soon-to-be conquerors.

"Since it appeared that they understood me and I understood them, I proposed my deal to them. I said, 'Now then, since I have dealt kindly with you, swear to me by the Lord that you in turn will deal kindly with my family. Give me a sign of good faith that you will spare my father and mother, my brothers and sisters, and all who belong to them, and deliver our lives from death' (Joshua 2:12–13).

"Surprisingly, considering what I'd heard about the Israelites, the two men agreed. They said that since I'd spared their lives, they would spare ours when the battle came. We agreed that I'd hang a red rope from my window and gather all my family into my house. Everyone there would be spared. However, if anyone in my family was not in the house at the time of battle, then he or she would be killed along with the other citizens of Jericho.

"After we reached our understanding, I dropped a rope for them to climb down from my window on the outside of the wall. I told them to go to the hill country and give the king's men time to give up their hunt. I suggested that after about three days, they should be safe. With that, they let themselves down to the ground and slipped away.

"I went to the kitchen, sat down, and laid my head on the cool wood of the table. My sister came in and asked if I was okay. I told her what had happened and what the plan was. She first looked shocked and then relieved that our family would be protected. She said that she would help spread the word to all our kin with strict instructions for silence about the plan. If any of the king's men learned of my agreement with the Israelites, then we would not need to worry about Joshua and his men. We'd all be slaughtered by our own people.

"We waited for the coming battle. The next events were truly odd and frankly frightening. The Israelites camped outside the walls of Jericho. We fully expected a battle with massive bloodshed as soon as they arrived. But no, it seemed they were performing some kind of ritual of worship or something. For six days, the warriors and all the Israelite people walked around the perimeter of our city … in silence. They carried an ornate box that seemed to have some religious significance to them. The only sound we heard was ram's horn trumpets blown by seven men whom I assumed were priests. It was eerie. Not a sound outside the city except for those irritating blasts from the trumpets and very few noises inside. For each of six days, the people and their box and their horns walked once around the perimeter of Jericho. At the end of each day, the Israelites settled into their camp for the night. Everyone was poised for battle.

"My family had gathered in my house. We watched with curiosity and some fear about what was happening outside our window. We checked a million times each day to make sure the red rope was still hanging outside to indicate which house was ours. We hoped and prayed to every god we could think of that the word of the Israelite spies was true. We wondered if their promise had been a way to get us all together so they could kill us.

"Things changed on day seven. On that day the Israelites began earlier than usual. They marched around the city six times, still in silence, but on the seventh time, every Israelite person shouted, and the trumpets blew and blew. The walls were breached as if they'd simply fallen down. My family and I huddled together while we heard the devastation going on outside around us. We heard screams and cries. We could hear items being smashed and cheers when someone captured one of the city's treasures. We were terrified.

"When a loud knock pounded on our door, we gasped. Some of the children began crying. I slowly went to the door while the knocking grew more insistent. I spoke through the door: 'Yes?'

"'Open the door!' I looked around in terror at my family and mouthed the words, 'I'm sorry.'

"Then again I heard, 'Woman, open the door. It's me, one of the men whose life you spared. I've come to take you and your family to safety.'

"You can't imagine the relief that I experienced when I heard that blessed statement. I quickly opened the door to let him in and bolted it behind him. He instructed all of us to leave the house using the rope just as he and his fellow spy had done. We helped all the older adults to leave first, then the children. All my sisters and brothers went next. Just before I left, I looked around my home, the one I had been so proud to own, and said a quick good-bye. I knew that our lives would never be the same again. The Israelite urged me to hurry, so I climbed out the window, and he came last. He told all of us to follow him to the Israelite camp, which we did. He could not allow us to enter because we were unclean, but he made sure that we were comfortable just outside the camp. We would gladly have slept in the open and eaten their garbage. We were just relieved to be safe and out of the destruction of our city.

"My family and I had now aligned our futures with the Israelites. We joined them in their food and worship practices. I eventually married an Israelite named Salmon. We had a son named Boaz who was the great-grandfather of King David. Who would have thought that an outcast of Jericho would have in my lineage both the greatest king Israel ever had and also the Messiah, Jesus of Nazareth?

"There is so much I can share with you about what I've learned that I hope you'll pass on. People judged me very negatively for what I did to take care of my family. Many people called me a prostitute, even the person who wrote down the story of the capture of Canaan by the Israelites and the author of the book of Hebrews. I suppose they must identify me that way. What I know is that I did what I had to do to take care of my family. There was no one else who would shoulder the burden that I willingly accepted. What I ask is that you not judge others harshly, especially if you do not know their circumstances. Who's to say that you would not have done the same thing?

"I also learned that people whom you may at first believe are enemies can actually be the people who protect your life. I could easily have given the spies from Shittim over to the king's men. My code of ethics said, however, that I would protect guests in my home no matter the personal cost. How tempting it is to do what is expedient for yourself rather than to care for those who are put into your life. I did not choose for these men to stay with me. They simply ended up at my house, and I assumed responsibility for their welfare. I encourage you to do the same.

"Taking this idea even further, because we moved into the world beyond Jericho, I learned that I might need to be responsible for people beyond my own flesh and blood. My initial motivation was to take care of my family. When we joined the Israelites and I married one of them, I realized that my worldview needed to widen. That is not always easy. My family and I had to learn new food customs, ways to dress, and ways to live together as a people. At first this was very scary, but when I look at my lineage, how glad I am that I followed my heart to care for people with whom I had no blood ties. I invite you to look at all the peoples of the earth as you would your blood kin and care for them in the same compassionate and passionate way. You too may make possible the life of a future world leader!

"You may want to develop your own personal code of ethics. In my time, I was supposed to swear allegiance to the king, but my code told me that the people staying under my roof were more important. Caring for my family required me to do things that nice girls did not do. Do I regret any of my actions? Not really, when I look at the outcome. Do I wish that my own people had not ostracized me? Of course. But then I may not have been as willing to hide the spies and help them escape, thereby ensuring the safety of my family. When I look back, I realize that my life turned out exactly as the holy God of Israel intended when I was created in my mother's womb. I hope you will comprehend that sometimes what seems so painful at the time becomes the best thing that ever happened to you. God's ways certainly are mysterious, as I learned when we all left Jericho.

"My life is a rich tapestry of intrigue, dedication to family, common sense, fearless actions, and faith in the holy God. May you be so blessed."

I looked at Rahab with admiration. She was truly remarkable, and I told her so. We sat companionably together for a while. Then she said that she needed to get back to her family.

"Thank you, dearest sister, for sharing your story with me. Blessings go with you."

Reflecting on Rahab's Visit

1. Rahab asked us not to judge others harshly, especially if we do not know their circumstances. She suggests that we might have done the same thing.

    + How do you respond to Rahab's statement about judging others? What are the challenges or barriers to not being judgmental?
    + Have you ever done something that surprised you when you did it? Why did you behave in a way that you did not expect?

2. Rahab admonished us to remember that people whom we may at first believe are enemies can actually be the people who protect our lives.

    + Do you agree or disagree?
    + Do you have an example that illustrates Rahab's point?

3. Rahab said, "How tempting it is to do what is expedient for yourself rather than to care for those who are put into your life. I did not choose for these men to stay with me. They simply ended up at my house, and I assumed responsibility for their welfare. I encourage you to do the same."

    + Does this statement challenge you in your own life or community? If so, how?
    + Does Rahab's journey stir up a story for you? If so, what?

4. Rahab implored us to look at all the peoples of the earth as we would our blood kin and care for them in the same compassionate and passionate way.

   - Who needs to be included in our world family? Who is left out?
   - What are the challenges of thinking about all the peoples of the world as our blood kin?

5. Rahab said, "Develop your own personal code of ethics. In my time, I was supposed to swear allegiance to the king, but my code told me that the people staying under my roof were more important."

   - What is your personal code of ethics?
   - Does your code always align with the political and governmental constructs of your community?
   - Do you want to make any changes to your code of ethics?
   - Where did your code of ethics come from?

6. Rahab said, "When I look back, I realize that my life turned out exactly as the holy God of Israel intended when I was created in my mother's womb. I hope you will comprehend that sometimes what seems so painful at the time becomes the best thing that ever happened to you."

   - Do you agree with Rahab? Why or why not?
   - What did you learn from listening to Rahab?

7. Rahab declared that God's ways certainly are mysterious, as she learned when she and her family all left Jericho.

   - Do you agree that God's ways are mysterious? Why or why not?
   - Does her story inspire you to action? If so, what? When? How? Why?

Chapter Eight

Rebekah—Family and Privilege

Genesis 24:1–28:5

Rebekah was the daughter-in-law of Abraham and Sarah, wife of Isaac, and mother of Esau and Jacob.

Several of my friends and I joke that we wish there was a book for how to parent adult children. There are plenty of books about being pregnant and about parenting babies and toddlers. There are even guides for dealing with teenagers. There probably are books for parents of adult children. We just need to find them!

I was sitting on the porch remembering a recent conversation among several of us with grown children. We had laughed, with a twinge of hurt, while we wondered what we were supposed to do. If we asked a question, we were sometimes accused of interfering. If we didn't ask a question, we might be charged with not caring. If we called, we were butting in. If we did not call, we must not love them. Should we talk with them every day? Once a week? Once a month? Do we wait for them to call us, or do we call them? What if they never call? We all agreed there were times when having grown children was wonderful because we could interact with them as friends might. Nevertheless, there were occasions when they seemed to want to be treated as dependent children. We felt lured into trying to function in the parental role of their earlier years. Were we to treat them as totally independent or as dependent upon our help and advice? The problem was we never knew which was which!

We agreed that we muddle through and that having a friend dealing with some of the same questions was extremely helpful. We also mentioned that we had thought it would be easier to be a parent when we got to this stage. However, we discovered that when our children left home, the issues and decisions just became different.

This discussion was one that came up frequently, often triggered by something one of our adult children did or didn't do. Just that day, a couple of us had met for lunch and spent most of our time listening to each other and offering advice or consolation. I was full of feeling because we all knew the joy, privilege, and confusion that loving a child can cause. The rocking motion felt almost like a mother's cradle for me that day.

Someone had joined me. I looked over, nodded, and waited. Finally she spoke.

"Hello, my name is Rebekah. I am the daughter-in-law of Abraham and Sarah, the wife of Isaac, and the mother of Esau and Jacob. I'm the grandmother of Jacob's children: Reuben, Simeon, Levi, Judah, Dan, Naphtali, Gad, Asher, Issachar, Zebulun, Joseph, Benjamin, and Dinah. I have other grandchildren as well by Esau: Eliphaz, Reule, Jeush, Jalam, and Korah. These last ones, though, I do not count too much since their mothers were either Hittite or the daughter of Ishmael, whose mother was Hagar. With all these grandchildren, one would think that I was a blessed grandmother, honored by such abundance. However, the reality is that I never saw any of Jacob's children. After Esau left for Edom, I never saw his children either. When I died, I was a broken old woman, laid to rest beside my husband, Isaac, and his parents, Abraham and Sarah. Jacob was eventually buried there along with his wife, Leah."

I must have looked somewhat dazed with all the names, because Rebekah said, "I'm sorry. I tend to ramble on. I hope I did not bore you with all my grandchildren. Their names are the only thing I have to hold to my heart. I hope that you can learn from my story so that you will not have the same ache."

I assured her that I wanted to hear her story and learn from her.

Rebekah continued. "My family is a very interesting family, to say the least. Abraham is Esau and Jacob's grandfather. With God's leading,

64

he left his ancestral home; suffered famine; and went down into Egypt where my twins' grandmother, Sarah, was passed off to Pharaoh as Abraham's sister. When Pharaoh discovered the ruse, he sent Abraham and Sarah away with slaves, animals, and many riches. Late in life, Sarah gave birth to the twins' father, Isaac—a total surprise. She knew that Abraham was supposed to be the father of great nations, but without children, she didn't see how that could happen. She took matters into her own hands when she gave Abraham her slave, Hagar, who bore a son, Ishmael, Isaac's older half-brother. Hagar and Ishmael were sent away to protect Abraham's legacy to Isaac. The second-born son, Isaac, therefore, received the blessing and birthright. At one point even that seemed in jeopardy, because God told Abraham to kill Isaac as a sacrifice, but once again God intervened and Isaac was saved to become the next in line for this promised great nation.

"Abraham was determined that his son would not marry one of those Canaanite women; therefore, he sent a servant on a trip to find the wife that God had in mind for Isaac. The servant prayed for a sign to know the one God had chosen. Sure enough, he found me. I responded as the girl who fulfilled the sign that the servant asked of God. Not only did I offer water to men and camels, I was also 'very fair to look upon' (Gen. 24:16) and was pure, as 'no man had known' me. I even offered the hospitality of my father's home when I said, without being asked, 'We have plenty of straw and fodder and a place to spend the night.'

"When the servant confirmed that I was indeed to be the wife of his master's son, I was given riches beyond my imaginings. I was overwhelmed with rings, bracelets, silver, and gold. My brother, Laban, who was the father of Leah and Rachel and ultimately the father-in-law of my son Jacob, closed the deal. My mother wanted me to wait with them for ten days to prepare, but Abraham's servant was in a hurry to return to Abraham. In what seemed no time at all, the servant packed me and my nurse onto the camels, and we rode into my future.

"We went to the Negeb to meet up with Isaac. He saw the caravan in the distance and began walking through the field to us. I asked who that was, and upon learning that he was my husband-to-be, I dismounted and covered my face. When the servant told Isaac that he had brought him a wife according to the instructions of Abraham, Isaac brought me into his mother's tent, where I became his wife. He loved me very much.

"The romantic beginning of our marriage soon turned to disappointment. I waited month after month to become pregnant, but no children came. Once again the promise of a great nation seemed in doubt. Isaac prayed to God for me, his barren wife, and the Lord granted his prayer. I became pregnant with not one but two children. This was not an easy pregnancy, and that's quite an understatement! The children seemed to battle within me during the entire nine months. There were times when I pleaded with the Holy One, 'God, why in the world did I want so badly to be pregnant? These babies are tearing my insides apart. Oh, God, please help me get through this.'

"And God said, 'Two nations are in your womb, and two peoples born of you shall be divided; the one shall be stronger than the other, the elder shall serve the younger' (Genesis 25:23). With the luxury of hindsight, I now know that I was given a hint about what would ultimately happen. I know I did not fully comprehend then what God's message meant. Some people who later tried to tell my story said that during my pregnancy, I went from being 'very fair to look upon' (Genesis 24:16) to being a conniving shrew. I'll let you decide about that for yourself. It's something I certainly have considered many nights as I tossed upon my pallet.

"Finally the twins were born. The first one to leave my body was Esau. Then came Jacob. Even at birth, they were physically different. Esau was red and very hairy, and Jacob was not. Jacob came out holding onto Esau's foot. I thought that was a sweet gesture. Some people who believe they know my story better than I do say that Jacob was already trying to usurp Esau's place. However, I thought Jacob, having spent nine months with his brother, was just trying to keep up, to make sure that he did not get left behind.

"This next part of the story is a difficult one for a mother to admit, but you may know of what I speak. I loved both my sons from the moment they were born. But ... but ... one of them was the child of my heart. I wish it were not so, but I loved Jacob better. His temperament and interests were more aligned with mine. Esau was more like his father.

"Does this make me a bad mother? Does this make me a horrible person? I wanted to love both my boys equally, but hard as I tried, I just could not. I wanted to treat my sons the same, but I just could not because of the ways our culture said things had to be done. I was a woman of my time. I urge you to think about what you do, the decisions you make, and the people you love simply because of the time and place you live in.

"As correct as it was according to the laws of birth order and inheritance, it did not seem fair to me that a matter of minutes—at the most—determined who got the birthright and the blessing. The children had shared everything to the point of their birth, but because Esau was born first, he, by all rights, received the inheritance. After their birth, almost immediately, the children received different things from Isaac and me, their parents. Isaac's favorite child was Esau. As Esau grew, he was what you might describe today as a man's man—a hunter and hairy. He brought his father food from his hunts. My favorite, as I've already mentioned, was Jacob, who liked to stay close to home.

"In my culture's way of thinking, Esau was the obvious choice for all good things. He was the firstborn, a skilled hunter, and his father's favorite. When you think about my son, Esau, I call for you to consider all the others, and possibly even you, who by virtue of birth, skin color, gender, socioeconomic situation, or education believe they deserve all the good things life has to offer. Do they simply take it for granted that life is good and they will be blessed with riches? Do they question their right to power, possessions, or prominence? Do they simply assume these things are theirs?

"In my time, we acted as if it were perfectly natural that the second or third born didn't have such blessings. Some people, like my Esau, did not know the challenges of not being blessed, of not having opportunities, or of not getting more than their fair share, at least until those things were taken away from him.

"By the reality of being the first to come out of my womb, Esau was the one who was destined to receive all our family's riches and hopes."

I interjected, "I understand what you're saying. Esau might be that person in the twenty-first century who says, 'I'm a self-made person. If I can do it, why can't that person over there that lives in poverty?'"

She looked at me as if she were expecting more, so I continued, "I guess I'd like to ask that self-made person, 'Do you use a computer in your work? Yes? Well, did you create the software that you use? Did you create the hardware that you use? No? Then how can you say you are a self-made person?'"

Rebekah beamed at me and exclaimed, "Thank you. I do not know the language about computers and software that you use, but you understand what I'm trying to say! Just because someone is the firstborn does not necessarily make him the one to know how to care for the entire family and the inheritance!"

She continued, "Jacob, my second born—by just minutes, I remind you—did not hunt. He liked to stay close to home. Some people even made fun of him because he didn't do the manly kinds of things his brother did. Later on, he worked very hard for years and years for Laban, his father-in-law, to obtain his wives, Leah and Rachel. Nevertheless, until he had to go away because of my deceitful act, he stayed close to me.

"The extreme rivalry that happened later was not evident as the boys were growing up. Esau and Jacob played together. They learned to share and to take turns. At times they were each other's best friend and worst enemy. They were twins, after all, never knowing what life was like without the other one there. One day Jacob was cooking. He loved to cook even though that was considered women's work. He *really* was not a young man who fit the cultural norms of our time. Esau came in from hunting and smelled the food. Esau, in his hunter's way, said, 'Let me have some of that red stuff, for I am famished.' I guess we've all, at one time or another, exaggerated a bit when we wanted to let others know how we're doing.

"As I've thought about what happened, this is how I understand it: These are two brothers who have spent their entire lives together vying for their parents' love and trying to best each other. So when Esau said, 'I'm famished,' Jacob came back with, 'What will you give me for it?' I heard Jacob and Esau say these same words many times throughout the years as they bickered over one thing or another. Jacob says he wants something, and Esau says, 'What will you give me for it?'

68

"Esau played the same game, except this time when he said, 'Give me food,' Jacob said, 'Sell me your birthright.' In the way that brothers banter, Esau said, 'Well, I'm dying anyway, so what does it matter? Okay, you got it.'

"'Swear.'

"'I swear.' This had become more than boys' playing. This was Esau's careless disregard for important things, things such as security, land, and prosperity.

"When Jacob told me what had happened, the seed for deceit was planted in my heart. I could not believe that Esau could so easily cast aside his inheritance. He did not deserve to carry on the great line promised to my father-in-law, Abraham. Esau also disregarded our traditions when he married two Hittite women, women who did not worship our Lord God. Esau had acted once again on his immediate desires without thought for the future and God's great promise of descendants as numerous as the stars. I knew I had to do something.

"One day I overheard Isaac ask Esau to go out hunting and bring back something savory to eat. He told Esau that he would then give him his blessing. That Isaac, always thinking with his stomach! He and Esau were definitely cut from the same cloth when it came to eating. However, thank the Lord that I overheard that conversation. I decided to help Jacob obtain Isaac's blessing for himself.

"I called Jacob to me and told him what I had heard. Jacob's face fell, but I said, 'I have a plan.' Jacob looked puzzled but agreed to do as I instructed him. He killed two goat kids so I could make Isaac the savory meal that he desired. Then I took one of Esau's fine garments and asked Jacob to put it on. This way, he would smell of his brother. I took the skin of the goats and put it on Jacob's hands and arms so he would be hairy like his brother. Isaac's eyesight was poor, and I hoped he would be fooled. Jacob was afraid that Isaac would figure out our deception and would curse him rather than bless him. I told him that if that happened, I would take the curse, not him.

"Praise the Lord, everything went as planned. Isaac seemed somewhat suspicious, because he asked Jacob—who he thought was Esau—how he managed to be back so quickly. Jacob replied that the Lord was with him. Isaac asked Jacob several times if he were truly Esau. Jacob said he was. I realized I was holding my breath while all this was going on. Finally Isaac took the food and wine, ate it, and then gave Jacob his blessing. At that, I took a large breath of relief.

"Within a very short time, Esau returned with joyous news about his hunt. He enthusiastically went to his father with his succulent gift. When he came into Isaac's presence, Isaac said, 'Who are you?' and Esau patiently replied, 'I am your first born, Esau.' He knew that his father was blind.

"At that, Isaac realized what had happened. He shook all over. He raged about the recent events. When he told Esau that he had just given his blessing to Jacob because he had been tricked, Esau puffed up with all his might and cried, 'Father, bless me too.' Isaac, with tears in his old faded eyes, said sorrowfully, 'I cannot, because I have been deceived and have already given my blessing.'

"Esau once again proved to me that he was not the man to carry on our family legacy when he blamed Jacob for stealing his birthright. My Jacob did not steal it. Esau gave it away. God's words to me when I was pregnant became true. The Holy One had told me, 'Two nations are in your womb … The one shall be stronger than the other, the elder shall serve the younger' (Genesis 25:23).

"I became fearful of what Esau might do to Jacob. A servant heard him swear that he would kill Jacob as soon as Isaac died. I went to Isaac and told him I was afraid that Jacob too might marry one of those Hittite women. Isaac agreed to send Jacob to my brother, Laban, to find wives within the family constellation. I never saw Jacob again. He married Leah and Rachel and fathered twelve sons and one daughter. His sons became the twelve tribes of Israel.

"In one way, my story has a happy ending. Jacob was indeed the man to carry on the promises of the Holy One. But in another way, my story is painful. After Jacob left to go to Laban's home, I rarely had any contact with him. I would hear from travelers about the family with its numerous sons, but Jacob and I never again had the close bond that we'd shared for all those years. Was this the price I had to pay for my deception? I suppose. I'm not the first mother to have loved deeply only to be bereft later on as that beloved child leaves for his or her own life. I had to remind myself that I had done my part in God's plan, but how I miss my boy!

"I continued to care for Isaac until he died. Esau finally realized how displeased we were with his marriages to Hittite women. He decided to marry Mahalath, the daughter of Abraham's son Ishmael. My one consolation is that Jacob gave instructions to be buried at Mamre with me, his father, and his grandparents.

"I have no wisdom for you. I am not proud that I loved one son more than the other. I am not proud that I deceived my husband. I *am* proud that I helped Jacob find and follow his God-given path. Maybe that becomes my charge to you. Do what it takes to help a child find the path that is his or her legacy. So many children are prohibited from being the leaders they can be because of poverty, abuse, neglect, the circumstances or places of their birth, or other barriers. People with power try to block their growth. Cultural norms define roles that may be limiting to people. Do what you can to remove walls. My role resulted in the twelve tribes of Israel. I guess I can be proud of that even as I mourn the loss of my own close connection with my son."

Beth's heart

Rebekah stopped talking. She dabbed at her eyes. She looked over at me to make sure I was still listening. She saw me wipe tears from my own eyes. All I had ever heard about her was her deceitful and scheming ways. Beside me sat a woman who had given up so much. Her sacrifice resulted in a great nation. All I could do was cry. Her motherly love touched my heart deeply.

We reached out to each other's hand at the same time. We held hands for a while until I realized that she was gone.

Reflecting on Rebekah's Visit

1. Rebekah said to think about what you do, the decisions you make, and the people you love simply because of the time and place you live in.

   - Do you make decisions or envision the world differently from the generation before or after you?
   - What kinds of decisions do you make based on where you live now?

2. Rebekah admonished us when she said, "Consider all the others, and possibly even you, who by virtue of birth, skin color, gender, socioeconomic situation, or education believe they … deserve all the

good things life has to offer. Do they simply take it for granted that life is good and they will be blessed with riches? Do they question their right to power, possessions, or prominence? Do they simply assume they are theirs?"

+ How does your skin color affect the quality of your life?
+ How does your socioeconomic situation affect the choices you have?
+ How does your education or lack thereof affect your life journey?
+ Does Rebekah's story challenge you in your own life or community? If so, how?

3. Rebekah lamented, "I'm not the first mother to have loved deeply only to be bereft later on as that beloved child leaves for his or her own life. I had to remind myself that I had done my part in God's plan, but how I miss my boy."

+ Does Rebekah's journey stir up a story for you? If so, what?
+ How do you respond to Rebekah's part in God's plan?

4. Rebekah said, "Do what it takes to help a child find the path that is his or her legacy. So many children are prohibited from being the leaders they can be because of poverty, abuse, neglect, the circumstances or places of their birth, or other barriers. People with power try to block their growth. Cultural norms define roles to people that are limiting. Do what you can to remove walls."

+ What are some of your community's limiting factors that prevent people from becoming who God intends for them to be?
+ What can you do to enlarge the opportunities for others?
+ What did you learn from listening to Rebekah?
+ Does Rebekah's story inspire you to action? If so, what? When? How? Why?

Chapter Nine

Rhoda—Mistakes and Surprises

Acts 12

Rhoda was a servant girl in the home of John Mark's mother, Mary. She was present when Peter came to the house after his escape from prison.

I am obsessively punctual. I like to arrive at speaking engagements about fifteen minutes ahead of time. When I drive to an engagement out of town, I leave with plenty of time to get lost and still arrive with time to spare. I still use a paper calendar so that I can have not only the time of an appointment but also my contact's phone and e-mail address along with other information pertinent to the occasion. If I were to lose that calendar, I would feel as if I'd lost my life!

I was heading out for a presentation and had allowed plenty of time to get there and still be about fifteen minutes early. As I was pulling out of my driveway, my phone rang. A voice on the other end said, "We're here waiting on you."

I said with full confidence that I had the time on my calendar at 9:00 a.m., and it was now 8:30. The voice informed me that the time was actually 8:30. I hurried and arrived fifteen minutes late rather than fifteen minutes early. When I returned home, I checked my calendar and realized that, indeed, my calendar said that I was to begin the presentation at 8:30. Not only that, I was to have brought along some information they needed. Since I had not done that, I e-mailed the document.

All in all, I'd goofed. I was not happy, but I told myself that no real harm was done. The group and I had had a good session together. I had apologized for my mistake and taken full responsibility for not looking more closely at my calendar.

Later in the day I went to the porch to think about all the things that had happened that day. I considered how I could have made the error about the time. I came up with several plausible explanations, but none of them altered the fact that I had messed up. I rocked and tried to give myself permission to let my mistake go rather than feeling bad because of the morning's events.

I was joined by a young woman. Almost as soon as I noticed her, she began talking.

"I'm just a silly girl. I'm even embarrassed to tell you what I did. I'll share my story so that you will be wiser than I was and know how to keep your wits about you. My actions just reinforced people's opinion that my head was always in the clouds and not really attached to my body. I hope you will learn from my … I don't even know what to call it … stupidity? foolishness? immaturity? shock? caving under pressure? lack of faith?"

I put my hand up with my palm facing her in order to slow her down and said, "Okay. I realize that you have a story to tell, but what's your name?"

"Oh my. See? I told you that I'm flighty, but I guess that's not so bad, since I ended up in the Bible. Now everyone knows what a silly girl I am." She began to fluff the skirt of her robe.

I repeated, "And your name is …?"

"Silly me. My name is Rhoda."

"Welcome, Rhoda. I'm eager to hear your story."

"Well, I was a servant girl in the household of Mary, John Mark's mother. You know John Mark? He traveled with Paul on some of Paul's evangelistic tours. Anyway, I worked there." She folded her hands, rocked in the chair, and began looking around the porch.

I prompted her again. "Rhoda, I'd love to hear how you ended up in the Bible."

"Oh, yes. Well, it's because I'm so silly. Everyone has told me all my life that I'm silly, so I guess I am—silly, I mean. So here's what happened.

"Peter had been locked up by Herod just before the Passover festival. We had heard that he was being kept under heavy guard. James, the brother of John and son of Zebedee, had already been killed with the sword as ordered by King Herod. We just knew that Peter would be next. We assumed the king would wait until the end of Passover, since he did not want to incite a riot while Jerusalem was full of pilgrims. Many people gathered at Mary's house to pray for Peter. The hum of prayer was constant from the moment we received word that Peter had been arrested.

"One night I heard a knock at the outer gate. I went to the gate and heard Peter's voice. I couldn't believe it. I was so happy I ran back inside to let everyone know Peter was standing at the gate. They just looked at me. They assumed I was being a silly girl again. They told me I was out of my mind. I said, 'No, Peter's at the gate!' They still did not believe me and said I was just hearing his ghost, even though they called it an angel. I still was adamant that Peter was standing at the gate. They finally heard some knocking and went to see who was at the gate at that time of night.

"And what do you know! Peter was indeed standing at the gate knocking. Just then I realized how stupid I had been—leaving Peter standing outside when he could have been picked up by the authorities at any moment. How could I have been so ignorant? I hope that you never do anything like I did, getting so wrapped up in the emotions of the moment that your brain just flies out of your head.

"They opened the gate to Peter, but he immediately told them to be quiet. I guess he did not want to arouse any suspicion. He waited until he was safely in the house before he told us what had happened. We sat listening and barely breathed. I stayed on the edge of the group because I was embarrassed at how foolish I had been.

"Peter had indeed been imprisoned and was heavily guarded. Four squads of guards were assigned to him. Herod did not want anything to happen to his prize catch. Peter said that he prayed all the time and felt surrounded by our prayers. The night before he was to be taken to Herod, the most amazing thing happened. Peter said that he was asleep with a guard on either side of him. There were also guards at the door. But something woke Peter up. He described it as a light shining in his cell.

"As Peter told his story, my eyes got bigger and bigger. He said that an angel appeared in his jail cell and told him to get up. Peter wondered how that might happen since he was chained, but when he stood up, the chains just fell off! The angel told him to put on his belt and sandals, wrap his cloak around him, and follow the angel. Peter said he thought he was dreaming. They walked past all the guards and out through an iron gate. They followed a lane until Peter realized that the angel had left him and he was suddenly alone.

"At this point in his story, Peter stopped and looked at each person sitting in the room to see if we all believed him. I guess our faces still looked stunned, because Peter said, 'Now I am sure that the Lord has sent his angel and rescued me from the hands of Herod and from all that the Jewish people were expecting' (Acts 12:11). He said that when he realized he was alone in the alley, he decided to come to Mary's house.

"I think he did not expect to encounter my foolishness. Can you imagine that I left Peter—Peter!—standing at the gate. Here he had been rescued by an angel only to be left knocking at the gate by a silly girl. I guess the angel expected more of me. That may be something to consider. Maybe we expect God to intervene when we are supposed to do something. I guess if the angel could make chains fall off and open iron gates, the angel could have opened Mary's outer gate. No, that job was mine, and I failed. Fortunately our holy God had a plan B when the other people in the house finally heard the knocking and let Peter in. God obviously does not do everything for us. We are supposed to do some things ourselves.

"I once heard someone say that God put the marble in the mountains but expected people to get it out and create beautiful buildings. I guess that was where I made my mistake. I did not fulfill my role in helping Peter to safety.

"Anyway, Peter was now safe with us. But the guards did not fare so well. We later heard that Herod was so angry when he learned that Peter had escaped that he personally visited the prison to see for himself. Then he had every one of the guards executed. I don't know what to think about that. It really was not the guards' fault that Peter escaped. That was the Lord's doing. However, they served the king, and I guess they had to live by the king's form of justice. I am confused about this kind of justice, but I'm just a silly girl, so what do I know? Maybe you can help me understand why people suffer for things they did not do.

"Peter left us and went to stay in Caesarea.

"As I think about all of this, I ask you to think about angels. I personally have never seen an angel, but then why would I? I'm just a servant girl. Have you ever seen an angel? Even though Peter's story seems impossible, I know it happened because I saw him with my own eyes.

"I also ask you to try to figure out ways to protect people who are innocent of things they are accused of doing. Those guards were simply doing their duty. They did not shirk their responsibilities. God, not them, helped Peter to escape. I feel bad about the guards even though they served the hated King Herod.

"Most surprising of all, realize that even stupid things like leaving Peter knocking at the gate can be important in the ongoing history of people living out their faith lives. Who would have thought that such a silly girl as I would have my name mentioned in the Bible? Possibly you have done something you believe is foolish. Maybe you feel as insignificant as I do. However, that very thing made me famous in an unexpected way. Who knows how these things work? I certainly don't. I'm just glad that I was a silly servant girl in the house of Mary, mother of John Mark."

With that, she jumped up out of the chair and bounded away.

Reflecting on Rhoda's Visit

1. Rhoda said, "I hope that you never do anything like I did, getting so wrapped up in the emotions of the moment that your brain just flies out of your head."

    + Have you ever had an experience similar to Rhoda's? If so, how did you feel?

2. Rhoda mused that maybe we expect God to intervene when we are supposed to do something. She said, "I guess if the angel could make chains fall off and open iron gates, the angel could have opened Mary's outer gate. No, that job was mine, and I failed."

    + How do you respond to Rhoda's assessment of God's activity?
    + Have you ever expected God to take care of something that was your responsibility? If so, why?

3. Rhoda was interested in angels. She said she had personally never seen an angel but did not expect to since she was a servant girl.

   + Have you ever seen an angel?
   + What do you think about Peter's experience with the angel? At first, he thought he was simply dreaming.

4. Rhoda asked us to figure out ways to protect people who are innocent of things they are accused of doing. She was concerned that the guards were simply doing their duty.

   + If you were a judge trying a case of the negligent guardsmen, what would be your verdict?
   + How do you respond to Rhoda's realization that the guards were punished for actions that were of God?

5. Rhoda said, "Realize that even stupid things like leaving Peter knocking at the gate can be important in the ongoing history of people living out their faith lives. Who would have thought that such a silly girl as I would have my name mentioned in the Bible? Possibly you have done something you believe is foolish. Maybe you feel as insignificant as I do. However, that very thing made me famous in an unexpected way. Who knows how these things work? I certainly don't."

   + Do you agree with Rhoda's assessment?
   + Does Rhoda challenge you in your own life or community? If so, how?
   + Does Rhoda's story stir up a story for you? If so, what?
   + What did you learn from listening to Rhoda?
   + Does Rhoda's story inspire you to action? If so, what? When? How? Why?

Chapter Ten

Sapphira—Greed and Lying

Acts 5:1–11

Sapphira and her husband, Ananias, were part of the early Christian community. They sold property, and rather than giving all the proceeds to the community, they held some of the money back. For that, they died.

I had just returned from making a gift in honor of a special event in a friend's life. I went directly to the place where I wanted the financial donation to go. I had a lovely visit with several of the staff members there. I was glad that I could do this special thing for my friend, but as always, I had to think about the appropriate amount to give. What size gift would be too large or too small? I knew that my friend would most likely never know the amount that I had given in her honor, but I would.

I went out to the porch to think about all the times in my life when I had to ask or help ask for money, whether in a nonprofit organization or in a congregation.

Part of my job as a nonprofit executive was to ask for contributions to help support our mission. I was very comfortable telling people of the fine work the organization did and then presenting a specific way they could get involved through a financial contribution or volunteering. I was rarely comfortable going to an individual and asking for a specific amount. Grants required that I submit a request for a defined amount of money, but I had difficulty doing that with individuals.

I also helped congregations ask for money on occasion when I worked with them during their stewardship campaigns. Usually this meant meeting with their leadership, discussing the true meaning of stewardship, and helping them become more comfortable when talking about giving. The congregations encouraged their members to pray about what God was asking each person or family to give. The leadership hoped that families would give more than just a formula percentage of income (before or after taxes? gross or net?). Whatever amount the family decided, the church leaders hoped the gift would represent to the family a sacrificial gift to God, the giver of life itself. After meeting with the leadership, I usually was the guest preacher on the Sunday when the members made their pledge commitments to God and the church.

Asking for money is often hard. I had to encourage, entice, and beg board members and others to help raise the funds that the nonprofit needed. A few board members loved seeking donations, but most were reticent. I understood their dilemma. Even when training was available about how to ask for gifts, some people still found it hard to discuss monetary donations.

In congregations, too, ministers found asking for money hard, because they feared that members would think the sermon was just about paying the preacher. Of course, that's not true—or at least it's only a tiny part of the truth. I think that's why it was easier—and safer—to invite me.

All of these things were rumbling around inside while I was still reviewing the adequacy of the gift I had made in my friend's honor. I noticed that I was no longer sitting alone on the porch. I looked over and saw a beautiful woman. I said, "Welcome to the porch. May I ask your name?"

She replied, "My name is Sapphira. If you know anything about me, it's probably not good. I certainly am not proud of what I did."

I answered, "Since I don't know what you're talking about, I'm very curious. I'd certainly love to hear your story. Maybe you will be able to teach me something."

Sapphira proceeded. "My name, Sapphira, means 'beautiful.' Many told me when I was growing up that my name was appropriate. More than once someone said, 'What a beautiful child.' My parents beamed, because they expected that I'd be able to make a very successful marriage.

"When it came time for me to wed, Ananias approached my parents. At that time, I did not know his name. I peeked at him from behind a curtain and was certain I'd never seen him before. I knew that I would have remembered him, because I certainly liked what I saw. He was pleasing to the eye. The quality of his robe indicated that he was a man of means. In a moment, I wanted more than anything to be this man's wife. I knew that my beauty would be an asset to him. I also considered that he'd be able to keep me in a fine manner. He would provide lovely gifts to me that would only enhance my beauty.

"I could not hear all the conversation. I knew that my father and Ananias were discussing my dowry and the marriage terms. My father related the entire conversation to me after the marriage arrangement had been finalized. He said that Ananias participated in a group that met in Jerusalem where Peter, a man known to be a disciple of Jesus, and James, the brother of Jesus, regularly taught and preached. Ananias wanted to make sure that my father did not object to his practices of faith. My father was never a very religious man. All he could see was his future son-in-law's obvious wealth. He said he had no objections to his daughter marrying a Jew who had joined this particular sect. After all, the name Ananias meant 'Yahweh is gracious.'

"The wedding celebration was wonderful. People partied long and with enthusiasm. Everyone complimented my parents on the auspicious marriage that their daughter had made. My wedding clothes were made of the finest materials available. I truly lived up to my name and made my family very proud.

"My marriage to Ananias was everything I had hoped for. He gave me beautiful things to wear and for our home. He bought property to enhance our holdings. I was very proud to be his wife. I was a little concerned about his involvement in this Jerusalem group. They were very serious about what they believed. All kinds of people began joining the meetings. I was not sure about some of the people who came, especially peasants and slaves. I was even a little suspicious of the man Peter. I had heard that he had once been a fisherman. I could certainly believe that because of the dialect he spoke and the way he dressed. The group was very important, however, to my husband, so I went along.

"One thing I liked about this gathering was that I was able wear my beautiful clothes to be seen and admired. I tried to act humble on the outside, but inside I glowed with the appreciation I thought the others felt. I believed that some of them were even jealous because their clothes were not as nice as mine.

"As this sect grew, it became known as a church—not a synagogue. I didn't care. Church, synagogue—it all seemed the same to me until the group made a significant change in how they took care of each other. All the believers decided that no one would claim private ownership of anything. What belonged to one belonged to everyone. They committed to providing for everyone in the church so that no one needed anything. People began selling some of their land and even their homes in order to give the proceeds to the church leaders, whom they called apostles.

"Well, I thought this was going too far. I wasn't about to give up my pretty things. People admired me, I thought, and I said so to Ananias.

"He replied, 'My beautiful wife, I love you dearly. You are the rose of Sharon and a lily of the valley to me. However, I must tell you that people do not admire your beauty when you come into the gathering spot with all your finery. They see you as haughty and proud. They question if you are a true believer. Some even have suggested that you should stay home and not attend the meetings with me.'

"When Ananias said those cruel things to me, I burst into tears and ran from the room. I picked up a pottery bowl and slammed it to the floor, where it broke into as many pieces as there are stars in the sky. I was hurt and angry. All my life I had lived with my beauty and the privileges it had given to me. I feared that Ananias would ask me to give up everything. I had to think what could be done about this change of circumstances.

"Later, when Ananias joined me on our pallet, I turned away from him and refused to talk with him. I did this for several days and nights while I thought about what I could do. Surely there had to be a middle ground where I could keep some of my pretty things and we could also provide for believers in the congregation.

"I could tell that Ananias was torn. He wanted to spoil me, his beautiful wife, but he was also growing more and more deeply committed to the message of the apostles. He believed that Jesus had been raised from the dead and was the long-awaited messiah. He believed we were to obey everything that Jesus taught, and that meant caring for the oppressed, the outsider, and the downtrodden.

"All my pouting and crying could not change his mind. He said his faith was too strong to ignore the teachings of the apostles. He also said, however, that he loved me with all his heart and that he wanted us to be happy like we used to be.

"I could tell that my distance was not pleasing to my husband, and I was scared. What if he decided to put me aside because I was not being the wife he wanted?

"I decided to prepare a dinner of Ananias's favorite foods. He was suspicious, because I had been unkind to him for several days. When he had completed his sumptuous meal, I said, 'My husband, I have not been a good wife. I have been thinking only of myself. I have ignored those poor believers who also are part of the Jerusalem church.'

"Ananias looked at me with curiosity and then a relieved smile. He said, 'You really mean that? If so, I've been thinking about selling that last piece of property I bought and then giving the proceeds to the church.'

"That was not exactly the way I had expected the conversation to go. I bowed my head, I think with a look of humility, and cleared the remains of the meal away. That night we once again slept as husband and wife. Well, I did not sleep. I lay awake thinking about what my next move could be.

"In the morning, I arose early. I dressed carefully, not too fancy and not too dowdy. I greeted my husband with a beautiful smile. I said, 'Dear husband, does the church require that you give everything to it? If so, what happens when we give away all your wealth? Will we become one of the families that the church has to take care of? This does not sound prudent. You owe it to the church not to become a burden on it. You want to be able to provide for the believers who need help. When you give away everything, you will no longer be able to fulfill this obligation.

"He looked at me and said, 'You are not only beautiful but also very wise. I will indeed sell the land that I chose. However, so that we will not become destitute and become a burden on the church for our livelihood, I will keep a portion for us.'

"I cast my eyes down and said, 'Dear husband, what did I do to marry such a brilliant and compassionate man as you?'

"By the end of the week, Ananias had completed the transaction. He was excited to be able to provide so generously for the church with the portion of the proceeds he was planning to lay at the apostles' feet. Almost immediately, he delivered the money to the church.

"I was not there, but knowing my husband as I do, I think he expected to be applauded for his magnificent gift. Ananias had not yet returned home, but I could not wait to experience what I assumed was Peter's happy reaction. I went to see the apostle and found out that Ananias had been there three hours earlier. I was confused about why he had not come back home to give me the good news himself. I decided that he must have had other business and that he planned to share Peter's joyful pleasure with me that evening.

"When I saw Peter, I was genuinely confused when he said, 'Tell me whether you and your husband sold the land for such and such a price' (Acts 5:8). I thought that Ananias had already been to the church until I heard Peter's question to me.

"I answered, 'Yes, that was the price.' I glowed with pride at the amount that Ananias and I had agreed we would give to the believers.

"Then Peter said, 'How is it that you have agreed together to put the Spirit of the Lord to the test? Look, the feet of those who have buried your husband are at the door, and they will carry you out' (Acts 5:9).

"I could hardly take in the shock of my husband's death before I too collapsed and died."

I looked at Sapphira with wide eyes. "You dropped dead simply because you did not give all the proceeds of the land sale to the church?"

She nodded. Then she said, "As much as I do not want to admit it, our deaths were the right thing to have happened. At first we rationalized how we could keep some of the money. We made a very logical decision, to our way of thinking. We believed we were extremely generous while making sure that we did not end up destitute. We thoroughly convinced ourselves of the rightness of our decision. Have you ever done that—convinced yourself that a bad decision was actually the correct one?

"And we lied. We lied not just to Peter but to God. We underdeclared the proceeds we got from the sale of the land. We were wrong. As believers, we were to think of others. How many times had the conversation included the teaching of Jesus to love the Lord our God with all our hearts, souls, minds, and strength and to love our neighbors as ourselves? I did not love my neighbors. I only loved myself and, of course, my husband.

"Some people believe our treatment was harsh. I do not think so. In order to preach and spread the gospel, the church truly needed the support of everyone who had resources. Our deceit hindered that work. I'm not sure that I could have ever given joyfully to the Jerusalem believers. I was too spoiled. But our deaths did serve as an example to others. They got scared. I have to joke now and say this was one powerful stewardship sermon. Its title could have been 'Give All or Die.' I honestly do not think we died because we did not give our all but because we lied about it. Sure, we may have been ostracized if Ananias had announced that he was not going to sell any of his property. He could have explained our decision with our rationalization that the congregation might need the sale more later on. We lied. We pretended that we'd given our all to the apostles for the preaching of the gospel when we had not.

"I suspect that people still do that—lie about their generosity, rationalize their nongiving decisions, or give with greedy hearts. I encourage you to give joyfully, with a full heart, and generously. If you can love your neighbor as yourself in your innermost being as I could not, you will live with love and exuberance in the grace and steadfast love of God, knowing the richness of walking the way of Jesus the Christ. You will not die literally (well, of course, at some date you will die, but in good time, not like my husband and I did). You will not die in your innermost being because your stinginess shriveled you up.

"When I think about how beautiful my life could have been had I been able to devote my entire being to the way of Jesus rather than to the surface beauty that I thought was so important, I grieve all that I missed. Please do not repeat my mistakes."

I stared into the distance, trying to take in all that Sapphira had told me. I glanced back over to where she was sitting, but her chair was empty.

Reflecting on Sapphira's Visit

1. Sapphira admitted that she and Ananias convinced themselves of the rightness of their decision.

   + Have you ever done that? Have you ever convinced yourself that a bad decision was actually the correct one? What happened next?
   + What kinds of arguments become plausible for rationalizing that bad decisions are actually good ones?

2. Sapphira said she suspected that people still lie about their generosity, rationalize their nongiving decisions, or give with greedy hearts. She encourages us to give joyfully, with a full heart, and generously.

   + Do you have an example of how giving joyfully enriched your life?
   + How does your family decide to spend its charitable dollars?

3. Sapphira said, "When I think about how beautiful my life could have been had I been able to devote my entire being to the way of Jesus rather than to the surface beauty that I thought was so important, I grieve all that I missed. Please do not repeat my mistakes."

   + Do you agree with Sapphira's assessment? Why or why not?
   + Does Sapphira challenge you in your own life or community? If so, how?
   + What did you learn from listening to Sapphira?
   + Does her story inspire you to action? If so, what? When? How? Why?

Chapter Eleven

The Witch of Endor—Compassionate Service

I Samuel 28:3–25

King Saul came to the witch of Endor for advice the day before he died in battle.

The weather was hot and humid. I took a glass of cold tea to the porch to see if I could cool off. It had been one of those days. It seemed that everywhere I turned, people wanted something of me. At times, I wanted to scream, "Leave me alone! Do it yourself."

I was especially galled when a person whom I really did not like implored me to help out with a problem. What made the request even more irritating was that the problem was caused by this person's actions— or more truthfully, by this person's inaction. Sure, I could have solved the problem without much challenge, but the situation just really made me mad.

I knew that this mad place was not where I wanted to be; therefore, I began trying to be grateful for other people—wonderful people—in my life. I mentally began a list. One person immediately came to mind. She was there to hold my hand and offer one of the most beautiful prayers I'd ever heard when I wasn't sure I could tolerate another minute of pain. I'd received devastating news about someone close to me. My friend was my God-given companion at the exact moment I needed her. I thanked God once again for this sweet angel of mercy.

Nevertheless, the day's events kept coming back at me. I was beginning to build up another wave of anger, which certainly did not help me deal with the summer heat. Just then I noticed I had a visitor. I looked over at a woman who was very strange looking. She did not look like anyone I'd ever seen before. Her clothing was shades of dark colors and hung loosely on her. Her hair was long and of a nondescript color. I couldn't tell her age at all. She looked both ancient and fresh as an adolescent.

I greeted her, "Hello. Will you please tell me who you are?"

"I am called the witch of Endor by some, and others call me the medium of Endor."

I thought to myself, *That explains your peculiar look*, but I said aloud, "You don't look like a witch!"

She smiled mysteriously and replied, "I will take that as a compliment."

I was absolutely fascinated. I continued, "I assume that you're mentioned in the Bible? I don't really remember any witches there. In Shakespeare, yes, but in the Bible?"

"Well, I'm there … in the Bible. King Saul consulted me."

With this, my anger was gone. I no longer felt the heat. I was entranced as I said, "That must be an interesting story. I'd love to hear it and learn what wisdom you have to share with me."

"I'll be happy to talk with you. I'll need to give you some background, though. Samuel had been called by God to be a judge and prophet for the Israelites. He led with God's guidance and kept us safe. In fact, while Samuel was leading us, the Philistines were subdued and did not enter the territory of Israel (I Samuel 7:13). Samuel and the people thought that his sons would take over when he was no longer able to lead. But those boys, Joel and Abijah? They were pitiful—more concerned about taking care of themselves than about guiding the twelve tribes of Israel. They took bribes and perverted justice. Because Samuel was getting old, the elders of Israel began to get scared about what was going to happen when he was no longer around.

"So what did the people decide? Well, they asked for a king—actually, they pleaded with Samuel for a king—since all the nations surrounding them had kings. Samuel did not think having a king was a very good idea. He told them they did not really understand what they were asking. A king would tax them heavily and conscript them to serve in the military. He reminded them that God surely did not want them to have a king, because they had God to lead them. Why did they need a king? But the people begged and begged. They were determined to have a king; therefore, God told Samuel to give the people what they wanted.

"God guided Samuel to choose Saul. Why did God choose this one person? Even though I am a medium and know things not known by others, I cannot fathom God's choice. Saul was stupid—in my humble opinion. This I could not say, of course, while Saul was alive, but this man had, shall I say, issues.

"For example, shortly after Samuel had identified Saul as the next king, Saul was supposed to wait for Samuel at Gilgal. He waited a week and then, rather than continuing to wait for Samuel, Saul proceeded to offer a sacrifice to God. When Samuel showed up and screamed, 'What have you done?' Saul said, 'When I saw that the people were slipping away from me, and that you did not come within the days appointed, and that the Philistines were mustering at Michmash, I said, "Now the Philistines will come down upon me at Gilgal, and I have not entreated the favor of the Lord"; so I forced myself, and offered a burnt offering'(I Samuel 13:12). What really happened is that Saul did not trust that God was with him. Samuel told him God's tough verdict: Saul's kingdom would not continue.

"Then Saul, stupid man, was told to destroy everything when he captured the Amalekites. Once again, he disobeyed and kept out all the good treasures because he wanted to offer them to God. Samuel had to tell him yet again that God was disappointed in him. Samuel's basic message to Saul was that because Saul rejected God's word, God rejected Saul as king.

"But Samuel kept trying. In a speech to the people, he said, 'For the Lord will not cast away his people, for his great name's sake, because it has pleased the Lord to make you a people for himself. Moreover as for me, far be it from me that I should sin against the Lord by ceasing to pray for you; and I will instruct you in the good and the right way' (I Samuel 12:22–23).

"Samuel was grieved and truly saddened along with God that Saul had been made king. The Lord God eventually instructed Samuel to anoint David as king behind Saul's back. When that happened, the spirit of God left Saul."

The woman paused in her story, allowing me to ask, "How do you know all this?"

She looked at me straight in the face as if she was thinking deep thoughts. Then she said, "You remember that I am a medium?"

"Yes, but—"

"Okay, I suppose you need to know that it was against Jewish law for those of us with special powers of insight and knowledge to live. The law said, 'You shall not permit a female sorcerer to live' (Exodus 22:18). The great king himself, Saul, had banished all the mediums and wizards from the land. That was especially curious, since Saul called Samuel a seer. I told you the man was odd. Maybe it was because of the headaches he had.

"Nevertheless, there were a number of us mediums around who lived as quietly as we could. Small groups of us would meet and share what information we had. We were careful never to come together in large gatherings, because we did not want to draw attention to ourselves. We lived in fear that someone, a friend or family member, might reveal our presence. However, we needed to know what Saul was doing since he had declared us to be unwelcome. We also developed ways to send messages or warnings to each other.

"Getting back to my story, when Saul discovered that David had been anointed by Samuel, he really began doing very strange things for a king. Rather than fighting our enemies, Saul spent much of his time chasing David in order to kill him. So instead of fighting people outside of our lands, Saul was fighting one of his own.

"When Samuel died, the tension between David and Saul became even worse. To David's credit, he could have killed Saul several times but spared him.

"David was a strategic warrior. He aligned himself with Achish in Philistia but continued to raid Philistine towns. Every time he went to battle, he lied to Achish and said that he'd been raiding towns in Israel.

"Saul heard that the Philistines were rallying an attack on him. He feared that David would be with the Philistines. He was scared. Since Samuel had died, Saul no longer had him to consult. Saul performed divination and paid attention to his dreams, but he received no answers. Then he told one of his men to find a medium who could advise him. It happens that the person he asked was my cousin, who knew about my gifts and had protected me. However, when his king gave him a command, my cousin's loyalty had to remain with his leader rather than his relative.

"Saul dressed as a beggar and came to see me one night. I was uneasy when I opened the door to this stranger and his two friends. He said he needed me to raise a spirit for him. My response was, 'Surely you know what Saul has done, how he has cut off the mediums and the wizards from the land. Why then are you laying a snare for my life to bring about my death?' (I Samuel 28:9).

"The man swore by God that no harm would come to me. I still did not admit that I was a medium, but I was curious. I asked, 'Whom shall I bring up for you?' (I Samuel 28:11). The stranger wanted Samuel.

"This I tell you: sometimes people ask you to do something, and that something feels like a trap. However, when you have the gifts to do what you are asked, especially when the person making the request seems in distress, you have to take a chance. In this case, I was risking my life, but I knew that I had to help this poor soul. God may ask us to do things that feel very risky, but since this stranger swore by the Lord, I just had to trust.

"I called out, and Samuel appeared. I got really scared, because I knew then that the stranger in my home was no mere peasant but King Saul. I screeched that he had deceived me. I fully expected him to pull his sword and put it through me, but he said, 'Have no fear. What do you see? (I Samuel 28:13).

"I described an old man wrapped in a robe coming up out of the ground. Saul knew that I indeed had seen Samuel, so he bowed low to the ground. And this is what happened next.

"Samuel said, 'Why have you disturbed me by bringing me up? (I Samuel 28:15).

"Saul spoke of his fear of the Philistines. He knew that God had turned against him because he could not get answers from dreams or prophets. Saul wanted Samuel to tell him what to do.

"Samuel was not happy. He told Saul what he'd already told him while Samuel still walked the earth. The Lord had turned from Saul because of his disobedience. Then he concluded his visit to Saul with these devastating words: 'The Lord will give Israel along with you into the hands of the Philistines; and tomorrow you and your sons shall be with me; the Lord will also give the army of Israel into the hands of the Philistines? (I Samuel 28:19).

"Then Samuel left."

The woman paused for a moment in her story before continuing. "I sat there not knowing what to do. This was terrible news that I had helped to deliver. I knew that now I would surely die. What happened next truly surprised me. Saul fainted. I am not sure whether it was from fear or hunger. His companions told me that he had not eaten all day or all night. I went to this pitiful man and said, 'Your servant has listened to you; I have taken my life in my hand, and have listened to what you have said to me. Now, therefore, you also listen to your servant; let me set a morsel of bread before you. Eat, that you may have strength when you go your way' (I Samuel 28:21–22).

"Saul finally agreed to eat. I killed the calf I was fattening up for a family celebration, and I baked bread. My grandmother had taught me that you always offer food to someone in need. You give them your best, not your leftovers. That was hard for me with this guest, since he could have killed me and had already sent so many of my friends away. However, I knew that my gifts of insight were for healing and not for hurting. That also meant my cooking was needed for help as well. Let that be a lesson for you. When you can ease someone's suffering, you do it, even though it may cost you some of your own well-laid plans.

"After eating and regaining his strength, Saul left. As it turned out, that may have been the very last meal he ever ate. Just as Samuel had told him, Saul and his sons died the next day. The Philistines killed Jonathan, Abinadab, and Malchishua. Saul was badly wounded. Rather than giving the Philistines the satisfaction of killing him, he fell on his own sword.

"I have thought long and hard about my interchange with Saul. He was, in many ways, his own worst enemy. And yet he was a man full of fear and disappointment. When Samuel abandoned him and told Saul that God had withdrawn God's spirit from him, the king was truly a broken man. My role at the end of his life was to give him answers that he desperately sought and offer him some sustenance for his body. I hope that my helping him with Samuel also provided food for his soul even though the prophecy came true the next day.

"I share my story with you because you never know when someone will need your very special gifts to help them. You'll be called upon to help others even at your own peril. You may even choose to go beyond basic assistance and, like I did, provide a splendid repast for someone who, under other circumstances, would be dangerous to you.

"One other thing: your gifts may not be appreciated. After all, Jewish law was harsh on people like me. And yet your God-given gift may be exactly what someone needs. When that person is someone of high power and authority, overcome your fear and listen to the voice of the Holy One. Use your gift for good and go beyond the merest requirements of duty. Give with love and compassion. Who knows? You too may be the last person on earth to offer compassion to this poor soul."

I could not speak when she finished. Her words moved me beyond all my expectations. The call to physically care for someone who could harm me was quite a challenge. I sat in my chair and matched my rocking rhythm to hers. In a few minutes, she said, "I have to go now. I have work to do."

And with that, I was once again alone on my porch.

Reflecting on the Witch of Endor's Visit

1. The witch said, "This I tell you. Sometimes people ask you to do something, and that something feels like a trap. However, when you have the gifts to do what you are asked, especially when the person making the request seems in distress, you have to take a chance."

   + Do you agree or disagree? Why?
   + Is the witch a good or bad character in the Bible?

2. The witch said that when we can ease someone's suffering, we are to do it, even though it may cost us some of our own well-laid plans.

   + Has someone ever put aside some of their plans to help you? How did you feel?
   + Have you ever adjusted your plans in order to help someone else? How did you feel?
   + Does this suggestion from the witch reflect the teachings of Jesus to you?

3. The witch said, "You never know when someone will need your very special gifts to help them. You'll be called upon to help others even at your own peril. You may even choose to go beyond basic assistance and, like I did, provide a splendid repast for someone who, under other circumstances, would be dangerous to you."

    -   What gifts do you have to share for the good of others? Do you have gifts of the head (planning, teaching, etc.); the heart (love, compassion, etc.); or the hands (actions, talents, etc.)?
    -   Are there dangerous people in your life whom God might place in your path so you can help them? Will you choose fear or faith?

4. The witch said, "Your gifts may not be appreciated ... And yet your God-given gift may be exactly what someone needs. When that person is someone of high power and authority, overcome your fear and listen to the voice of the Holy One. Use your gift for good, and go beyond the merest requirements of duty. Give with love and compassion. Who knows? You too may be the last person on earth to offer compassion to this poor soul."

    -   What advice can you give to someone to help them overcome their fear in order to follow God's leading?
    -   Have you ever been the last person to interact with someone just before they died? What kinds of feelings did you have? Was that a holy or horrible time, or both?
    -   Does the witch challenge you in your own life or community? If so, how?
    -   What did you learn from listening to the witch of Endor?
    -   Does her story inspire you to action? If so, what? When? How? Why?

Chapter Twelve

The Woman Caught in Adultery—
Judgment and Strength

John 8:1–11

A woman was caught in adultery and brought before Jesus for stoning. However, she walked away.

A friend of mine told me at lunch that day about her early days as an ordained minister. She said that following her call had proven to be very difficult. She had felt called to parish ministry, but since she was a pioneer as a woman clergyperson, many congregations did not want her as their minister. She was criticized for not having an authoritarian voice. She said she understood that meant that she didn't speak with a man's voice. She was told that the church could not call her because the women wondered how men in the church could come to her for counseling. She retorted to me, "What did they think I would do, seduce their husbands? Women have been going to male preachers for counseling for generations!" She said that she was criticized for the shoes she wore if they had open toes or when her jewelry was anything other than small pearl earrings. She was told, "That was a nice sermon—for a woman!"

Eventually a very small church called her. She was willing to work for the meager salary they could pay. As she gained experience and the world began to change, she moved to a larger congregation. She said that she was forever grateful to the first little church that took a chance on her.

All the members eventually believed that God truly meant for her to be their minister. Everyone grieved when she left, even those who were most opposed to her at first.

As I was relaxing on the porch after a day full of meetings both interesting and boring, I thought about those women who carved out a path in ordained ministry for all the women who followed. I was grateful to the friend who had talked with me that day. I even offered a prayer of thanksgiving for her ministry and witness throughout the years. Just as I said amen, I realized I had a guest on the porch.

I looked over and said, "Hello."

She smiled and nodded acknowledgement of me. I continued, "I've enjoyed many guests here who have told me their stories, encouraged my growth, and challenged me in exciting and provocative ways. I assume that you are here to do the same?"

She said, "Yes, I suppose I am."

She began, "I am a woman truly blessed. I could have been dead had it not been for the rabbi Jesus. Have you ever heard about him? He was different from any other rabbi that I knew about."

I smiled and remarked, "Yes, I've heard of Jesus. In fact, I'm a follower."

"Oh, good. Then maybe this story won't sound bizarre to you. Of course, *I've* never thought it was bizarre. I just think it's a miracle."

I replied, "I still do not know who you are, dear lady."

"Well, you don't need to know my name. After all, it's not given in the Bible. I'm usually known as the woman caught in adultery."

I'm sure that my face registered surprise. I said, "I've read about you. Welcome to my porch."

"Really, you're welcoming me? Even though you know who I am? I'm usually known as a sinner."

I chuckled as I quipped, "Aren't we all?"

"But have you ever done anything that could get you killed?"

I answered, "I don't think so, but I'm not so sure getting caught in adultery is worth the death sentence either."

"That's because you're living in a different time than mine. The law from the Torah said that 'if a man commits adultery with the wife of his neighbor, both the adulterer and the adulteress shall be put to death' (Leviticus 20:10). I was even told that the rabbi Jesus said, 'Whoever divorces his wife and marries another commits adultery against her; and if she divorces her husband and marries another, she commits adultery' (Mark 10:11)."

I said, "That's harsh. But I don't remember that a man was brought with you to Jesus. Only you were brought before him. That's not usual, is it?"

"As I said, the times were different.

"Let me tell you a little more about myself. I was divorced. Once again I will teach you some of the law from the Torah. The law says, 'Suppose a man enters into marriage with a woman, but she does not please him because he finds something objectionable about her, and so he writes her a certificate of divorce, puts it in her hand, and sends her out of his house; she then leaves his house and goes off to become another man's wife. Then suppose the second man dislikes her, writes her a bill of divorce, puts it in her hand, and sends her out of his house (or the second man dies); her first husband, who sent her away, is not permitted to take her again to be his wife after she has been defiled; for that would be abhorrent to the Lord' (Deuteronomy 24:1–4).

"That's what happened to me. My first husband divorced me. You may have already noticed that I am well-versed in the Torah. My father studied Torah, and I often sat with him while he pored over the parchments. When his eyes began to fail him, I would read the holy words to him. As I read, I learned more and more. Certainly women were not to be knowledgeable in the law as I was. I tried to keep my learning secret from my husband. I suspected that he would not be pleased to have a wife like me because I would be a disgrace to him. Nevertheless, one day he just made me so mad that I quoted the law to him. He stopped talking immediately and looked as if I had slapped him. I hung my head and moved back to my cooking pots. However, he grabbed my arm, turned me around to face him, and said, 'What did you say?'

"I repeated the law. He stomped out of the house. I finished preparing our meal and thoroughly cleaned the house. I did not want to give him anything else to be displeased about. When he came home, he was silent while we ate our supper. We went to bed in our usual way, and I believed that my slip had not caused major harm.

97

"The next morning my husband told me he had visited the rabbi and told him what I had said. The rabbi confirmed that I had indeed correctly stated the law. My husband asked how I knew of such things. I told him honestly about my father and me. He listened to my story and left the house. When he came home later that day, he handed me the certificate of divorce. That was that.

"I returned to my father's house and told him what had happened. At first he was irate that my husband had treated me in such a way. Then he was angry with himself for allowing me to learn beside him. His rheumy old eyes watered up. I threw my arms around him and cried, 'No, Papa, I wanted to learn. Do not blame yourself. I am so happy that you taught me our sacred laws.'

"My father touched my cheek, smiled weakly, and said, 'Let me think on these things. I will make a plan for my precious daughter.' With that, he sent me to help my mother with our meal.

"The days passed, and I began to heal from the hurt of being cast aside by my husband. I had truly begun to love him—the way he laughed, how he smelled, the way he took care of me, and how he ate everything I placed before him—even the burned foods! I missed him and was ashamed of the divorce. What helped me through this difficult time was once again being able to read Torah with my father. We resumed our practice, but my father had to cut our sessions short several times because his health would not allow him to spend hours studying as he once did.

"One day he called me to him. He said, 'All is well, my daughter. One of my friends will marry you. He's not quite as old as I. His wife died recently, and he is lonely. He knows about your love of Torah and even hopes that you will teach him since he can no longer work. Nevertheless, he can take care of you and will be kind to you.'

"I knew that my father did this out of love for me. I thanked him even while my heart hurt. My father was concerned about what would happen to me after he died, and this was his way of taking care of me. I hugged my father, in part so he could not see the pain and disappointment in my face, kissed his neck, and whispered, 'Thank you.'

"The wedding was simple, not lavish as my first one had been. I moved into my new husband's house and began taking care of him. Thank the Lord, his children were all grown, so it was just the two of us most of the time. I did love his daughter, who would help me with the housework and cooking when she came to visit her father. She always brought her two children, a boy of seven and a four-year-old girl. I enjoyed having them around the house. I had to console myself that her children would be the only children in my life since my husband was so old.

"My father was correct when he said my husband was a kind man. My husband asked me to share with him my knowledge, which I did with joy. He would sit and hold my hand while I taught him. He told me that he loved to watch my face light up when I talked about passages that I especially liked. I told my father before he died how very grateful I was to him for finding this man to be my husband.

"We had a wonderful life for about eight years before my husband died. His daughter and I by that time had become very close, almost like sisters. When her father died, she and her husband invited me to live in their home. I thought of her as my sister and her children as my niece and nephew. I certainly loved them as my own.

"One day I was in the market and saw my first husband. He had changed very little. My heart did a flip, and I realized that I still had feelings for him. He did not see me then, but I noted what day of the week and time of day I'd seen him at the market. I began to go to the market at that time every week. Sometimes I'd see him and other times I would not.

"I talked to my stepdaughter about my feelings. She at first looked astounded that I would still have such feelings for a man who had divorced me. However, like a loving sister, she finally encouraged me to have my little fantasies. She and I knew that he and I would not speak in the market, because such behavior was forbidden.

"Little did I know that my first husband had seen me on that first day in the market and regularly watched for me. He did not approach me because he knew that would jeopardize my reputation. He figured he'd already done enough damage there.

"One day I came home from a walk to find my stepdaughter's husband talking with my first husband out in front of our house. I know that I gasped aloud, because both men looked in my direction. I lowered my eyes and went—I should say ran—into the house. I asked my stepdaughter if she knew what they were talking about. She said she did not, but she would eventually find out from her husband and let me know.

"Several days went by before my stepdaughter was able to tell me about my first husband's visit to her home. She said that he had realized what a mistake he had made. When he'd seen me as the wife of my second husband, jealousy had raged in his heart. Now that my husband had died, he wanted to have me back.

"Even though we knew this was not possible, we were drawn to each other. The feelings of our youth ignited again. I kept up my marketing schedule, and we would just happen to meet at a booth. We did not say anything to one another, but our eyes spoke to each other. Occasionally, our fingers would touch as we both reached for the same pomegranate. We maintained propriety.

"My stepdaughter saw how I became alive again. She had become concerned after the death of her father when she saw me withdraw from life. Now she knew that I was happy, because once again I sang songs of our faith and whispered lines from the Torah.

"We talked about how impossible my situation was. We knew that it was forbidden for a husband to reclaim a woman he had divorced if she had remarried. We also knew that some teachers did not enforce certain of the Torah laws as strictly as others did. We began to discuss how my husband and I might be reunited.

"Until we figured out a plan, my stepdaughter's husband would invite my husband to his home to discuss business—at least that's what they both said in public. Little did we know that we were being watched. Some of the religious leaders knew of my knowledge of the Torah and were not happy that I, a woman, was as astute as they were about the law. When my first husband began coming to the house where I lived, they decided that now might be a time to 'put me in my place.'

"One evening, when my husband was at the house, my stepdaughter and her husband decided to take a walk in the cool of the evening. My husband fully expressed his feelings for me once again. My heart leaped like a deer. We touched each other's hands and repeated the sacred words of marriage that we had said so many years ago. In our hearts, we were married.

"The four of us became less cautious. We enjoyed each other's company.

Celebrating Shabbat together each week was especially meaningful. We often walked outside under the cloak of darkness to enjoy the breeze and to see more than the inside walls of the house. Unfortunately we were noticed one evening by some scribes and Pharisees. They had been observing us for several weeks. This particular evening, however, they saw my husband reach over and touch my hand. After our walk, we all four went back home. My husband left in the early-morning hours when no one could see him leave after an evening of much pleasant conversation among the four of us.

"We all went to bed feeling loved and happy.

"But early the next morning, there was a loud knock on the door. A score of scribes and Pharisees were standing there with extremely stern looks on their faces, their arms folded across their bodies and their power exuding from their robes. The spokesman said, 'Give us the adulteress!'

"My stepdaughter's husband, who opened the door, looked at them with puzzlement. 'What are you saying? What adulteress?'

"The haughty man said, 'Your step-mother-in-law—the one who speaks Torah—the one who was seen being touched by her former husband. Send her out immediately!'

"By now, my stepdaughter was standing behind her husband. She motioned for me to stay hidden as she went to the door. She too looked astounded at such a lie from the religious leaders. The scribes and Pharisees were unrelenting. I scrambled to change from my night clothes, but before I was fully dressed, two of the men pushed into the house, found me, and pulled me out into the street. They roughly pushed me ahead of them. I had no idea where we were going, but I was terrified. I could see them picking up rocks along the road. Since they had called me an adulteress, I knew that they planned to stone me. I just did not know where they were planning to do this foul deed.

"Then I saw the Temple ahead. I thought, *Surely they are not going to stone me there!* However, we walked closer and closer, and their handling of me became rougher and rougher. Before I knew it, I was standing in front of a rabbi surrounded by all these angry men. I was ashamed, because my hair was in tangles and my clothes barely covered me since I had not had sufficient time to dress after my night's sleep. I hung my head and tried to cover my breasts and legs as best as I could.

"The spokesperson said to the rabbi, 'Teacher, this woman was caught in the very act of committing adultery. Now in the law Moses commanded us to stone such women. Now what do you say?' (John 8:5). I cringed to hear the verdict, 'Stone her!' but I did not hear those words.

"I waited and wondered what was happening. I only looked down and not at any of the people standing around. I noticed out of the corner of my eye that the rabbi was leaning toward the ground. I could see him without looking up. When he bent down further, he took his finger and wrote something in the dust. I was not close enough to read what he wrote.

"Even while the teacher was writing, the crowd kept pounding him with questions. It seemed as if I was some kind of test for him. Finally he stood up and said, 'Let anyone among you who is without sin be the first to throw a stone at her' (John 8:7). And then he bent down again to the ground and began writing.

"I tensed to feel the first stone hit me. I waited but felt nothing. I stood still with my head hanging down. Waiting ... waiting ... but no rocks came. I was scared to move even my eyelid. I stood as still as I possibly could. I reasoned that if I moved even a hair, the stones would come flying. I continued to wait ... wait.

"I heard a stone fall to the ground, but it landed nowhere near me. And then I heard another and another drop. The noise of the crowd grew less and less. I continued not to move. I could see shadows on the ground seemingly moving away from me. I still was braced for the first stone, but nothing came.

"Finally the rabbi spoke to me. When I heard his voice, gruff yet smooth, I looked up into the warmest eyes I have ever seen. They were not handsome, but they were full of love and moved me beyond anything I can express. He said, 'Woman, where are they?' (John 8:10). For the first time I looked around and was astounded to discover that the angry crowd had vanished. I looked back at him with questioning eyes.

"He said, 'Has no one condemned you?' (John 8:10).

"I looked around again to make sure that I was not imagining the scene and said, 'No one, sir' (John 8:11).

"He replied, 'Neither do I condemn you. Go your way, and from now on do not sin again' (John 8:11).

"I began to leave and then looked down at how I must have appeared with my hair and clothing all awry. As I looked around to see who was staring, I noticed my stepdaughter coming toward me carrying a cloak. At that moment, I burst into tears. I turned to say thank you to the rabbi, but he had moved on. My sister covered my body, and we went back home."

My guest looked timidly at me, and I realized at that moment that I had been holding my breath. I let out a big sigh. She seemed to relax into her chair. For much of her story, she had seemed to be in that faraway place. She slightly shook her head and said, "I learned in the next few days that the rabbi's name was Jesus. When I went to the market, I began to hear stories of this man. People repeated his words and told of his healing and feeding people.

"I know that it's hard to explain, but in this man, Jesus, I felt as if I had seen a glimpse of Yahweh, the God of Torah. I knew that I no longer wanted to be with my first husband. Even though I still had feelings for him, I knew deep in my heart that he would never understand my love of Torah and learning. I also knew that this Jesus would understand and know more about me than I could ever know about myself. I told my stepdaughter that I was leaving her and her family and would follow this man, this rabbi, this Jesus, wherever he went. Have you ever experienced such a passion?

"My stepdaughter begged me to stay. She asked me if I knew what I was doing. I had to honestly say that I had no idea what was in my future. I simply knew that I had to join the other women who followed him and help him in any way I could.

"I encourage you to follow your passion. My father opened the world of Torah to me, and although my knowledge caused me pain, I cannot imagine living without the wisdom I have gained through my studies. If it were not for Torah, I would never have found Jesus, my Lord and my Savior. I also plead with you to defend those who need defending. The authorities were concerned about me because I was a woman who knew Torah. They found a way to publicly discredit and humiliate me. Don't let that happen to others just because they may be different or may not comply with the general rules of how things are done. When you experience another chance at a fulfilling life, grab it and hold on tight. When I say that Jesus is my Savior, I mean that in the most literal sense. He kept me from being stoned to death. With this new freedom, I knew that my life had changed forever, and I wanted—no, I needed—to follow this man."

I said, "Dear lady, you inspire me. Thank you so much for telling me your story. I appreciate learning more about you as a woman rather than just as a pawn in the disputes between Jesus and the religious authorities."

She nodded her head and was gone.

Reflecting on the Woman's Visit

1. The woman admonished us to follow our passion.

    + What does following your passion mean to you?
    + Are your passion and your God-given call the same thing?
    + What role does fear play in following one's passion?

2. The woman said, "Defend those who need defending."

    + Who in your life or community needs defending right now?
    + Where would you have been in the crowd surrounding the confrontation with Jesus?
    + Who has defended you in the past?

3. The woman instructed, "Don't let others be publicly discredited and humiliated just because they may be different or may not comply with the general rules of how things are done."

    + Who are the different ones in your community? How are they discredited or humiliated?
    + Does the woman challenge you in your own life or community? If so, how?

4. The woman said that when we experience another chance at a fulfilling life, we are to grab it and hold on tight.

   + Do you agree or disagree?
   + What are the challenges and opportunities of a second or third chance for a fulfilling life?
   + What did you learn from listening to the woman caught in adultery?
   + Does her story inspire you to action? If so, what? When? How? Why?

Bonus Chapter

Lady Wisdom: Proclamation and God's Way

Proverbs 1–8

Wisdom appears throughout all scripture and is personified as a woman in the early chapters of Proverbs.

I was sitting on the porch thinking about a woman who very proudly told me of her owl collection. She had more than two thousand owls, many of which were gifts to her. She had collected piece by piece an exquisite set of owl-inlaid dishes. Her drawer pulls were owls, the upholstery around her house used fabrics with owls, and she even wore a gigantic owl ring.

Just a few nights before, I had had a dream about an owl. In it, there was a small owl in a bird cage in the rear passenger seat of my car. Because the backseat was quite full with other things, the cage was level with the window, which was rolled down. The cage door got open somehow, and the owl flew out. I was devastated. Then the owl said, "Beth, you can't box me in."

As I rocked in my chair, I meditated on the meaning of that dream. First I thought about what owls might mean or symbolize. Owls often connote wisdom—I guess because their eyes make them look wise. As I thought about the dream, I realized that the owl symbolized God for me. God is wise, so the owl's words were God's to me at that time. I cannot box God in.

I was trying to discern ways that I was indeed limiting God in my life. I was also thinking about wisdom because I use that word a lot in my poverty-education work. I was filled with questions about God and about wisdom. How was I limiting what God could and would do in my life? How was I trying to keep the cage doors closed? What does wisdom really mean? What does it mean to be wise? Does it mean knowing the right thing to do at all times? Does it mean listening for that small voice of God when I interact with someone else? Does it mean being able to keep my own counsel and being calm and satisfied with that? Does it mean paying attention to when and how I'm trying to box God in?

I was just about to get up and go into the house to grab a dictionary to look up the definition of wisdom when I noticed a being in the other rocking chair. That's the only way I can describe what I saw. The shape was female, but there was a glow, a brightness that was not quite human and made the—what shall I say … person?—indistinct around the edges. I wasn't sure if I was in the company of a woman, an angel, or even God.

I asked very meekly, "Who are you? More importantly, what are you?"

The voice of the being answered, "I can understand that you do not know who I am. I am not like the other women who have visited with you on the porch. They have rich stories in the Bible and therefore are easy to relate to as women. I, on the other hand, have hints about me throughout all of scripture. There are specific references to me, especially in Proverbs, but I don't have the luxury of narrative tales. I am known by a variety of names. In Hebrew, I am called Hokmot. In Greek, I am called Sophia. Others call me Lady Wisdom. I prefer the last name. You may call me Lady."

I looked more closely. The being was taking on a more defined shape. She still was not fully embodied as Rebekah or Priscilla had been, but still I could tell I was talking with a female. When she identified herself, though, I became somewhat uneasy. Here was wisdom personified! She has sometimes been vilified in certain religious circles as if she were trying to usurp God's place. I wasn't sure that I wanted to have this being with me. What if someone found out? I know that women in the past have lost their jobs because they found in Lady Wisdom new ways to think about God and also to claim the wonder of wisdom for their own lives and the world. Even though I was intrigued, I was still nervous. However, I was raised with manners, so I said, "Welcome, Lady."

Lady Wisdom said, "I can sense that you are a little uncomfortable with my presence. I understand. Let's open the doors of that cage a bit first."

I was surprised that she knew about the cage. I wondered how she knew my dream until I remembered that she was Wisdom!

She said, "I am not separate from God, creator of the universe; Jesus, savior of the world; or the Holy Spirit, comforter and advocate. I am not a goddess; nor am I a fourth person of the triune God. However, I *am* one way of understanding a little bit of the holy God."

I nodded, but she could tell that I did not understand yet what she said.

Lady Wisdom continued. "Let me try to explain. I'll have to use some Bible verses to make my point. Here comes the professor side of me as wisdom! In Luke 11:49–51, the gospel writer says, 'Therefore, also the wisdom of God said, "I will send them prophets and apostles, some of whom they will kill and persecute."' Notice that I, the wisdom of God, said the part about sending prophets and apostles. Yet in other gospels, I am not mentioned, and these words come straight from Jesus's mouth. The Luke version means that some people try to force me to become the female equivalent of Jesus. I am not. I am in Jesus as wisdom—and we all know that Jesus was very wise. As we push the doors of that cage open a bit, you can discover in Jesus a very biblical and feminine part of what it means to be the savior of the world. It means to embody wisdom. What do you think of that?

"There are some other verses that add to the confusion. First I'll quote the verses specifically about me, Lady Wisdom, in the Roman Catholic Bible. Sirach 24:19 says, 'Come to me, you who desire me, and eat your fill of my fruits,' and Sirach 51:23 states, 'Draw near to me, you who are uneducated, and lodge in the house of instruction.' Don't these sound a lot like what Matthew reports that Jesus said in 11:28b–30: 'Come to me, all you that are weary and are carrying heavy burdens, and I will give you rest. Take my yoke upon you, and learn from me; for I am gentle and humble of heart, and you will find rest for your souls. For my yoke is easy, and my burden is light.' These parallels of Jesus's words and those attributed to me have confused men and women through the ages."

I replied, "Okay, thank you, Lady, but you're losing me."

She said, "I understand. I'm just giving you some thoughts to help you open the box that you've got God in. Let's try just one more. Listen to these words about me in Proverbs 8:22–31: 'The Lord created me at the beginning of [God's] work, the first of [God's] acts of long ago. Ages ago I was set up, at the first, before the beginning of the earth. When there were no depths I was brought forth … When [God] established the heavens, I was there, when [God] drew a circle on the face of the deep, when [God] made firm the skies above, when [God] established the fountains of the deep … when [God] marked out the foundations of the earth, then I was beside [the Lord], like a master worker; and I was daily [God's] delight, rejoicing before [God] always, rejoicing in this inhabited world and delighting in the human race.'

"Okay, these words were specifically about me, Hokmot, Sophia, Lady Wisdom. Do you recognize a familiar ring to them? Think."

There was silence while I considered Lady's question. Then I lit up and said, "This sounds like the first verses of the Gospel of John where John says, 'In the beginning was the Word, and the Word was with God, and the Word was God. He was in the beginning with God. All things came into being through him, and without him not one thing came into being' (John 1:1–3)."

Lady Wisdom clapped her hands and exclaimed, "Good answer! You understand! I am trying to open the cage doors so that you and others can more fully appreciate and worship the triune God. Because I, wisdom, was at creation, the whole plan becomes richer and fuller. Because I was embodied in Jesus, he becomes more than the way he is often portrayed. He is wisdom that is as old as creation itself. I can also enhance your understanding of the Spirit, who is often called the Advocate or Comforter. Now really, don't wisdom, advocacy, and comforting all belong together? Knowing about me is just another way to know about the awesomeness of the triune God."

I said thoughtfully, "I think I understand what you're trying to tell me. After all, the Bible uses a number of female metaphors to help us understand the Holy One. I remember Jesus saying, 'How often [O Jerusalem] have I desired to gather your children together as a hen gathers her brood under her wings, and you were not willing' (Matthew 23:37). And the prophet Hosea depicts God as a feisty mother bear when God says, 'I am the Lord your God … I will fall upon [those who forgot the Lord] like a bear robbed of her cubs' (Hosea 14:4, 8)."

"Yes, you're getting it. When you get to know me, you also know more about the God you worship. Okay, we've begun to open those cage doors a little. Now let's talk more about how visiting with me, Lady Wisdom, might enrich your life, if you choose to embrace my teachings. John J. Collins once called me an 'attitude to life, based on understanding.'

"Now I'll tell you who I am and what I did and continue to do. I cried out in the street and raised my voice in the square. I did not call out just to those who were chosen. I called out to everyone. I did not preach from a pulpit. I shared in the street. I called people to be fully human. My message was about instruction; insight; wise dealing; righteousness; justice; equity; shrewdness to the simple; knowledge; prudence to the young; gain in learning; acquiring skills; and understanding proverbs, words of the wise, and riddles. You will recognize that this, too, is how God acts in the world—calling out in the street, leading people to be fully human. My fruits, wisdom's fruits, are safety, living in harmony, and shalom or peace.

"I taught that wisdom was better than silver or gold. Wisdom, fullness of life, lasts beyond those trinkets that people place such value on. Every good path you walk allows fullness of life to come into your heart. Gaining true knowledge will be pleasant to your soul. Being prudent will bring security to you. Increasing your understanding of things in life that have depth, value, and meaning will give you a sense of being protected, of God guarding you. Wisdom, the very being of me, brings that fullness of life that you yearn for. When you are prudent, you have understanding. When you have understanding, you are knowledgeable about things that matter. When you are knowledgeable about things that matter, you walk in God's way. When you walk in God's way, you enjoy your life. And when you enjoy your life, this is the best gift I, the wisdom of God, can offer."

She paused to let all these things settle into my mind. After a few moments, she continued. "I know it's confusing. I am both a concept and, at least in the book of Proverbs, a person named Lady Wisdom. So what am I?

"Hmmm. Let's try it this way. If you need to dress up to go an important meeting, do you sometimes imagine a woman you admire and think how she would dress for this meeting? What you are doing is personifying the traits you admire in her and trying to make them yours.

"Well, that's kind of like it is with me. When you call on me, Lady Wisdom, you are calling on the best traits of what it means to be human. You have insight, love, peace, and safety. When you hold my hand, you are avoiding the seven things mentioned in Proverbs 6:16–19 that are hated by our Lord God. They are haughty eyes, a lying tongue, hands that shed innocent blood, a heart that devises wicked plans, feet that hurry to do evil, a lying witness who testifies falsely, and one who sows discord in a family."

I almost jumped out of my chair with insight when I said, "Oh my, Lady Wisdom, these sound like the Ten Commandments. 'Honor your father and your mother. You shall not bear false witness. You shall not murder.' And so forth."

"You are correct. My message is the same message you hear from God every day when you are willing to listen. I offer you a connection with God in a way that may be more down to earth than you sometimes hear about. Wisdom and grace go hand in hand. And God, this God of love, tells of me and the worth of my words throughout the entire scriptures. Righteousness, shalom, and peace that passes understanding are part of me. I am not separate from the full story of the Bible. Sometimes I may be more hidden. At other times, I may be a little more approachable. My words are ordinary and not fancy. I tell you of God—Creator, Redeemer, and Advocate or, if you prefer, Father, Son, and Holy Spirit.

"I am mystery and I am ordinary. I am woman. I am words, and I am more than words can describe. I am in the heart of God, and I want to be in your heart. You cannot touch me as you could Joanna when she visited. You cannot easily see me as you could Rhoda when she giggled here on the porch. And yet I am here. I am there. I have been part of the God story since the beginning of time and will continue to be present whenever people live in the fullness of their lives and help create opportunities of fullness for others. When people live fully as disciples of the risen Lord, they are living the life that I call them to from the streets and the city's open spaces.

"So what is my challenge to you? Now, my child, listen to me: you are happy when you keep my ways. Hear instruction and be wise and do not neglect it. You are happy when you listen to me, watch daily at my gates, and wait beside my doors. For whoever finds me finds life and obtains favor from the Lord; but those who miss me injure themselves; all who hate me love death (adapted from Proverbs 8:32–36).

"My ways are the Lord's ways. Never forget that. Never worship me. I am only a small magnifying glass to help you better worship the Lord God. Praise be God's name. Don't try to box God in. Live in the fullness of the life that you have been given by the holy Lord. Follow in the ways of Jesus. Abide in the Spirit. Shout all of this in the streets so that everyone can experience this wonder and gift."

With that she vanished with the wind, but I felt sweetness in my heart that had not been there before.

Reflecting on Lady Wisdom's Visit

1. Lady Wisdom said, "Listen to me: You are happy when you keep my ways. Hear instruction and be wise and do not neglect it. You are happy when you listen to me, watch daily at my gates, and wait beside my doors."

   + Do you agree or disagree?
   + What is your opinion of Lady Wisdom?

2. Lady Wisdom taught that her ways are the Lord's ways. Never forget that. Never worship her.

   + Do you agree or disagree?
   + Does Lady Wisdom expand your faith perspective or limit it?

3. Lady Wisdom said, "Don't try to box God in."

   + In what ways do you box God in?
   + What might you do to expand your understanding or relationship with God?

4. Lady Wisdom suggested that we live in the fullness of the life that we have been given by the holy Lord.

   + What does fullness of life look and feel like to you?
   + In what ways do you recognize God's actions in your life?

5. Lady Wisdom told us to follow in the ways of Jesus.

    *   How would you describe following in the ways of Jesus to another person?
    *   Is there someone in your life who models walking in the ways of Jesus? If so, who is it? How does he or she model that for you?

6. Lady Wisdom asked us to abide in the Spirit.

    *   What does this mean for you?
    *   Are there certain practices that help you abide in the Spirit?

7. Lady Wisdom said, "Shout all of this in the streets so that everyone can experience this wonder and gift."

    *   Does Lady Wisdom challenge you in your own life or community? If so, how?
    *   What did you learn from listening to Lady Wisdom?
    *   Does her story inspire you to action? If so, what? When? How? Why?

Afterword

Who knows if more women will come? After Lydia came, I thought no more women would visit. After a time, Lady Wisdom came and was followed by the others whose stories are in this book. The women continue to teach, embrace me with their wisdom, and challenge me. They open worlds of insight and give gifts to share with others.

Many other people—flesh-and-blood people, both men and women—have come to the porch to talk, share a meal, cry, or laugh. It continues to be a holy place. I wish for you a porch of your own and friends to embrace you with calls to action. When you have sensed your call, I encourage you to follow it with all your heart, soul, mind, and strength.

Other Women Who Have Visited the Porch

You can read about the visits of other women listed below in my book *Conversations on the Porch* (Bloomington, IN: iUniverse), 2011.

Eve—Blame and Grief

Sarah—Promises and Joy

Hagar—Abuse, Forgiveness, and God's Presence

Leah—Settling for Less and Caring for Others

Rachel—Challenges and Rewards

Shiphrah and Puah—Doing What Is Right

Miriam—Exuberant Celebration and Being Number Two

Deborah—Resolving Conflict

Levite's Concubine—Abuse and Sacrifice

Hannah—Yearning and Promises

Bathsheba—Authority and Nurture

Tamar—Victimization and Accountability

Huldah—Trusting and Speaking God's Truth

Naomi—Perseverance and God's Goodness

Ruth—Hope and Expectation

Vashti—Claiming One's Power

Esther—Acting with Courage and Wisdom

Daughters of Zelophehad—Confronting the Status Quo

Elizabeth—Claiming Your Dream

Mary—Pondering and Heeding God's Call

Anna—Knowing and Praising

Mary of Magdala—Being Blessed and Truth-Telling

Woman Who Hemorrhaged—Choices

Syro-Phoenician Mother—Calling for What Is Right

Woman Who Was Bent—Joining Jesus in Healing

Woman at the Well—Crossing Artificial Boundaries

Sister Mary—Following Your Heart with Loving Acts

Martha—Hospitality and Faithful Living

Dorcas—Reaching Out with Your God-Given Gifts

Lydia—Networks of Support and Refusing to Be Silenced

About the Author

Beth Lindsay Templeton, founder and CEO of Our Eyes Were Opened, Inc., is a public speaker, Presbyterian minister, and writer. For almost thirty years, she worked with both the have-nots and the haves at United Ministries, a nonprofit in Greenville, South Carolina. Since 2012, she has focused on a ministry with the haves so they can enlarge their thinking about people who live in poverty in order to decrease judgment and increase compassion. She works with congregations, schools, universities, medical facilities, civic groups, and businesses in Greenville and around the country. She is a graduate of Presbyterian College and Erskine Theological Seminary. She and her husband have three married sons and four grandchildren.

For more information, visit www.oureyeswereopened.org or www.bltempleton.com

2015
1991
———
24

Charlton Heston
(Jacob) Deborah Kerr

Made in the USA
Lexington, KY
21 December 2014